London Transport
1933-1962

London Transport 1933-1962

Michael H. C. Baker

First published 1996
Third impression 1999

ISBN 0 7110 2480 4

Published by Ian Allan Publishing

an imprint of Ian Allan Publishing Ltd,
Terminal House, Shepperton, Surrey
TW17 8AS.

Printed by Ian Allan Printing Ltd,
Riverdene Business Park, Hersham,
Surrey, KT12 4RG, England.

Code: 9902/2

Front cover: Preserved No NS1995

Back cover, top: Metropolitan Bo-Bo
locomotive No 14 seen at Baker
Street in 1961.
John Glover collection

Back cover, bottom: Silver R stock
and red Q stock in adjoining
platforms at Wimbledon. *Colour-rail*

Contents

Introduction

London Transport 1933–1962

I gave up collecting London bus numbers at the end of 1950 when I decided there was practically nothing but STLs and members of the RT family to record. I suppose it had something to do with the disappearance of the last STs and LTs, types which I had known all my life. Forty-five years on this seems a rather odd decision for I had a great liking for the STL, the successor of the ST and LT and which, as the most up-to-date standard London bus, I considered the bee's knees, the cat's pyjamas. This decision didn't lessen my interest in London buses, or trams, trolleybuses and trains for that matter. And if I didn't mark off numbers in my *abc* any more, I made a mental note of each batch of RTs which arrived, spanking new, to operate one of our local routes. Local was Croydon. But buses also operated into the town from Elmers End which was also pretty local and, a bit further afield, Catford, Bromley and Sutton, which were all outer suburban. We also got buses from closer in to the West End and the City from Streatham, Norwood, Old Kent Road, Nunhead, Camberwell and from the other side of the river, Chalk Farm. Then there were all the Country Area garages which sent their green double-deckers and single-deck Green Line coaches into Croydon, Chelsham, Godstone, East Grinstead, Dunton Green, Reigate, Crawley, Dorking, Guildford, Leatherhead, Hemel Hempstead, Amersham and Tring. Pause for breath; then on to tram depots at Thornton Heath, Telford Avenue and Brixton Hill and, sometimes, Purley, and finally two trolleybus routes whose vehicles lived at Carshalton and Hammersmith. All of which goes to show how such a wonderfully rich variety could not fail to engage the interest of any schoolboy remotely aware of public transport.

Many of us with an interest in public transport keep an eye out in the cinema for familiar buses passing behind the leading lady, and London, featuring probably more than all other cities in the kingdom put together, provides a rich harvest. Who doesn't know that familiar shot — particularly familiar around now as I'm writing this at the height of the VE-Day 50th anniversary celebrations — of a roof-box STL in Parliament Square in 1940 amongst a convoy of tanks? Hollywood, especially in black and white days, often passed off the most outrageous artefacts as genuine London vehicles, but one film which did get it right was the Fred Astaire, Ginger Rogers classic, *Top Hat*. Fred is driving Ginger across Westminster Bridge in a hansom cab and they pass in a brief but fascinating sequence, NSs, LTs, STs and an E3 tram on a Kingsway Subway service. The E3 is fitted with driver's screens and, *Top Hat* being released early in 1935, this feature and the liveries suggest these second unit scenes must have been filmed around 1933-4 when our book opens.

Within these pages we record the types, the changes, the liveries, the contractions and expansions, some of the people and a few personal reminiscences of the more than 30-year history of the largest urban transport undertaking in the world.

Michael H. C. Baker
July 1996

Below:
Southgate station, on the Piccadilly Line extension to Cockfosters, under construction. *Topical*

1933

The London Passenger Transport Board (LPTB) came into existence on Saturday 1 July 1933, less than three months after the bill setting it up had received the Royal Assent. It created the largest passenger transport operating organisation in the world. A total of 9,500,000 passengers was carried daily. For some areas of its operations great changes were in store; one thinks initially of the replacement of the trams by trolleybuses, but such diverse aspects as architecture and publicity would also come to the forefront. The underground and tube networks would expand, and buses and coaches, powered by diesel in future rather than petrol, carrying the London Transport name would penetrate far into the countryside of Kent, Surrey, Sussex, Middlesex, Buckinghamshire, Hertfordshire and Essex. Its operating area of some 2,000 square miles was defined as extending between 20 to 30 miles from Charing Cross.

Although a huge number of operators were absorbed by LT, many were very small, sometimes one-man only businesses. Inevitably it was the few big ones, the London County Council (LCC), the Underground Electric Railway Co and its subsidiary, the London General Omnibus Co (LGOC), which were to influence policy. There was a mixture of continuation in some areas and innovation in others.

For the trams 1933 was a year which suggested they might just have a future. The previous year the LCC had completed updating all its trams by fitting upholstered seats downstairs and at least partly upholstered ones upstairs. In the spring of that year tramcar No 1 emerged from Charlton Works. This splendid vehicle was based on the HR2 of 1930 but considerably more modern. It had concealed interior lighting, separate heated driver's cab, air and magnet brakes, air-operated doors, and was to be the prototype of a new generation of trams. In 1931 London United Tramways (LUT) and the Metropolitan Electric Tramways (MET) had put into service what was perhaps an even more revolutionary tram, the Feltham, or UCC class. No less than 40ft 6in long over fenders, these tremendous vehicles also had air-operated doors at back and front — allowing fast boarding and alighting — air and electromagnetic brakes, and ran so smoothly that they could coast considerable distances with power off. Both No 1 and the 100 members of the Feltham class were in truth in advance of any bus then in operation and there is evidence of preparations to build many more of them. In some respects both No 1 and the Felthams were still ahead of any other PSV when they were withdrawn from the streets of London in 1951-2 and sold for further service in Leeds.

Unfortunately most of the 2,465 (plus 165 in store) London trams were ancient and out of date, although still quite serviceable. While no tram services were withdrawn in 1933, the success of the Kingston area trolleybuses put into service by the LUT in 1931 had convinced LT that this was where the future of electrically powered road vehicles lay. Nevertheless just one day after LT came into existence a virtually new tram entered service, on 2 July 1933. This was No 1370. 'Virtually' needs some amplification, for its

origins are complex in the extreme. It had started out as LCC Class M car No 1446, dating from 1910 and was a four-wheel version of the standard E1 class bogie car. Most of the Ms (not the LCC's most successful tram because their riding could be uncomfortably nautical), were withdrawn in 1932 but three were converted to ME3 bogie vehicles. No 1446 was the third of these. It was given a brand new top deck — virtually identical to that of No 1, although the number and destination screens were different — flush lower deck sides, an aluminium-framed windscreen, and Hurst Nelson bogies. However, just before it was ready to enter service, an E1 car, No 1370, crashed outside the Oval, probably because the driver was trying to catch a glimpse of one of Jack Hobbs's last innings. This was deemed a write off; the money for its replacement was credited to the rebuilding of No 1446 which assumed No 1370's number. The story doesn't end even there, for some parts of the original 1370 were salvaged and were used up in yet another new, very similar car, No 2, which took up work in February 1935.

January 1933 saw the entry into service of the double-deck bus which was to be the London standard until the war. This was STL1. It wasn't a pretty vehicle. Its body was a development of the Bluebird LT Renown six-wheeler and ST Regent four-wheeler, but it did not share their handsome proportions. This was because it managed to squeeze 60 seats into its 26ft length. Until the previous year 25ft had been the maximum length allowed for four-wheel chassis and the 49-seat ST had been the standard Central Area double-decker. The upper deck of the STL projected ahead of the cab, being in line with the radiator and, as there was virtually no slope back or front, 34 seats were squeezed in upstairs, 26 downstairs. Lightweight materials were used wherever possible to keep the laden weight down to 10 tons, and whatever the original STL lacked in elegance, its design showed much originality. It was well built; indeed, one of the bodies lasted on a much later chassis until 1954, 21 years being a remarkable lifespan for a London bus in those days, particularly one which had suffered nearly six years of wartime neglect.

Another variety of STL was also in production in 1933. This was the Thomas Tilling version. Thomas Tilling, one of the most famous names in the British public transport industry, had been operating buses in London since 1847. Although keeping its independence it had been a member of the London

Left:
Oxford Street in late 1933. A brand new 'leaning back' STL on route 6 bound for Hackney Wick loads up outside Selfridges ahead of an LT on the 15. Both carry the legend 'General' as worn in LT's first months. *Author's collection*

Below:
Former Tilling STL80 from Catford Garage on the 36. Years of practice have removed all danger of the conductor losing his grip and dignity as he assumes standard nonchalant pose for rounding Marble Arch. *LT*

Right:
55, Broadway, the hub of the world's greatest urban transport system. *Topical*

Left:
Tram No 1 outside Holloway depot on a special working. It ran from this depot until 1938 when it was transferred southside to Telford Avenue. This picture was taken during a postwar visit to its old haunts. *IAL*

Below:
Tram No 2 in postwar days at the Catford terminus of the 52. The elegant top deck is somewhat compromised by the crude fitting of the windscreen to the dash. *IAL*

Right:
Two NSs give way to a tall-funnelled steamer at the West India Docks. *Author's collection*

Below right:
No 2376, an archaic looking former LUT U-class bogie car of 1902, heading towards Hampton Court on route 57. *Author's collection*

One bus which appeared wearing the title General, even though it wasn't completed until August 1933, was STL203. This was a 56-seater, the standard number for so many highbridge double-deckers of that period. It differed in many other respects from its immediate forebears and was well on the way to the standard STL. It was not yet there because its front, although more pleasing than that of the first LGOC STLs, sloped back and was not entirely smooth, and it had a petrol engine. The back was a fine piece of design, curving out gently from the base and then equally subtly to the roof line and the domed roof. In this respect the standard STL had been reached and in the author's opinion was more elegant than either the RT or the RM. This batch was completed with the entry of STL252 into service in November 1933, and was immediately followed by STL253, which was very similar but had a smoother frontal appearance.

On the Underground rebuilding of stations — Chancery Lane on the Central Line for example — continued. The final stage of the Piccadilly Line tube surface extension from Finsbury Park from its last but one station, Enfield West, to its impressively modernistic enclosed terminus at Cockfosters, designed by Charles Holden, was opened on 31 July. At that time tube trains were painted, like buses and trams, in a red and off white livery, unlike the all-red of modern surface stock, as the larger Metropolitan and District Line trains were known.

1934

While changes certainly took place in 1934, in retrospect it was a relatively quiet year, when the indelible image which LT was to impose on public transport in and around the capital was being honed and perfected but was yet far from evident. A new numbering system for all routes, except trams, and based on the old General one but much refined, was introduced in October. 1–199 were for Central Area, red, double-deck routes, 200–290 for Central Area single-deck routes, 291–299 for night routes, 300–399 for Country Area routes north of the Thames and 400–499 for Country Area routes south of the river.

Not all the independents out in the country areas had yet been absorbed and several were taken over at the beginning of the year by Green Line; the last on 22 February. The most important was the fleet belonging to Edward Hillman, who also operated an airline. Based in Romford — the airliners operated

Omnibus Pool since 1914. This tied it in very closely with the LGOC and some of the vehicles it operated were actually owned by the General. This applied to its STLs. However few members of the public would have realised this for they wore Tilling livery and carried Tilling-designed bodies which, beyond being double-deck and totally enclosed, bore scarcely no other resemblance to the LGOC STL. The first Tilling STL predated the first LGOC STL by three months, coming out in autumn 1932, and 17 were in service by the end of that year, leaving the remaining 63 to be produced between January and June 1933.

One of the most curious features of the first months of LT operation was that its buses carried the title 'General'. This was not because they had not got round to painting on the new title but because, for some reason, it was policy to use this title for new vehicles, ex-Thomas Tilling and other independents, even though the legal lettering proclaimed the owner as the LPTB.

Right:
The pioneer Leyland Cub, C1 working the 237 when new. *Author's collection*

Below:
Bedford BD5 working from WA garage on the 397. *Pamlin*

from Croydon — 300 employees and 65 Gilford coaches came with the garage.

Production of STLs continued apace throughout 1934 as it would until September 1939. The earlier ones were virtually identical to those of the previous year, although there were some variations within the group, notably in the fitting of preselector gearboxes to many. They had more powerful, secondhand petrol engines, removed from 1931 era LTs. These were replaced on the LTs by diesel engines, but 11 of the next run of STLs had diesel engines (of a smaller size than those on the LTs).

The first of what we can reasonably define as the standard STL, No 609, took up work from Hanwell garage in November, 1934. Not only was the diesel engine now standard but the body was extensively redesigned. Gone was the previous flat front and in its stead was a most elegant, gently sloping, totally modern one. Internally the design was equally well thought out and lightweight, tubular aluminium framed seats, scarcely different to those still familiar in Routemasters, were introduced on some later buses of this batch. An anachronism was the absence of a cab door, insisted upon by the Metropolitan Police, and a generally pretty primitive set up inside the cab with no instruments and a bulb horn.

A very different batch of STLs, Nos 1044–55, entered service in April and May, 1934. Although only 12 in number they became quite celebrated and lasted with LT for almost 20 years. They were front entrance, lowbridge buses with all-metal bodies of MCW provincial type design built at Weymann's Addlestone factory — in their final years some would operate from Addlestone garage. However they were

intended to work from Godstone on the 410, Reigate to Bromley route and this they did until 1950. Handsomely appointed inside, with a sliding door, they were popular with both passengers and enthusiasts. Like many other country buses at the time they were at first known only by the registration numbers.

Four buses which AEC hoped would revolutionise LT's attitude to the double-decker, but didn't, entered service in 1934. These were Q2-5, Q1 being a single-decker which had been operating since 1932. The Q, with its side-mounted engine, full front, entrance ahead of the front wheels and smooth, streamlined appearance, was indeed a bus for the future and when compared with the NS, several hundred of which were still at work in London, it showed what enormous strides had been made in bus design in 11 years. Indeed one cannot think of any comparable period in the history of the motorbus where there had been such obvious progress. Q2/3 had front entrance 56 seat Metro-Cammell bodies which, except for minor features bore little resemblance to the STL, while Q4/5 had similar looking Weymann bodies, but with the important difference of a central entrance and staircase and power operated sliding doors. The first two were painted red and soon became a familiar

sight in central London, taking up work, after a brief period in the suburbs, on the 52 Victoria to Mill Hill. Q4/5 were painted green and were sent to work the 406 between Kingston and Redhill. In the summer of 1937 Q2/3 were repainted green and were banished to the country and with the outbreak of war all four were taken out of service, there being no resources to keep such experimental vehicles on the road. LT does not in any case seem to have had much enthusiasm for the double-deck Q, although, as we shall see, it successfully operated the single-deck version in both Central and Country Areas and as a Green Line coach. Many of the double-deck Qs features were to be eventually taken up by the bus industry but the vehicles themselves were sold after the war (except for Q3 damaged in an air raid and broken up) and worked for a little longer with their new owners.

Only one new single-decker entered London's vast fleet in 1934. This was a Leyland Cub, a forward control design and the smallest in that firm's vast range of passenger vehicles. Numbered C1 it seated 20 passengers and was painted red and sent to work from Hornchurch garage, being transferred to the Country Area in 1935 and painted green. Originally fitted with a petrol engine, it was given a Perkins diesel one the following year. The neat, well proportioned body was designed and built at Chiswick, being instantly recognisable as such, a miniature version of standard London practice of the time.

The Underground, like other areas of the LT empire, was biding its time in 1934, waiting for what was shortly to come. On the District Line a new station was opened at Upminster Bridge in December.

1935

In 1935 LT unveiled its New Works Programme. Britain was still deep in the Depression which followed the 1929 Wall Street crash and although the British government was nothing like as courageous or enterprising as the Roosevelt administration in the USA in attempting to alleviate unemployment and re-start the economy, it did provide a modest amount of investment for public works and it guaranteed the £40 million loan which LT and the main line railway companies needed. The latter were involved for part of what was planned was the extension of the underground system out into the suburbs to the east and west either parallel to or over the tracks of the GWR and the LNER. We will look at each of these schemes as they were completed.

Equally important, and perhaps of more immediate general impact, was the announcement of the end of London's tramway network. With hindsight it may seem that this was inevitable, for the tram had reached its heyday around the time of World War 1 and with the great increase in speed and, above all, reliability and flexibility of the motorbus, many systems had already closed. These, however, were relatively small and many of those serving the great cities, Glasgow, Liverpool, Leeds and Sheffield in particular, were being re-equipped with fast, comfortable, streamlined cars and sometimes allowed to operate, in the suburbs, over reserved tracks. They seemed to have a future

and it is possible that if the Felthams and LCC No 1 had been given a chance to prove their worth, that the tram's extinction in London would have at least been postponed. To have expected the reprieve to have lasted until the 1980s and the revival of Light Rail is clearly a pipe dream for only Blackpool kept its trams operating through the 1960s and 1970s, but I am suggesting that the demise of the London tram might not have happened as early as it did.

Nevertheless LT considered that the trams had sufficient time left for 1,000 of them, the entire former LCC E1 class in fact, to be rebuilt, although by August 1935 when the official announcement was made, this had been reduced to 250. In the event even this proved too optimistic, only 154 being rebuilt, including four of the relatively modern HR2 cars and four equally modern ex-Croydon Corporation ones, these being virtually identical to the LCC E1. They were given new roller blind route and number indicators recessed into the panelling, flush fitting sides, windscreens, while internally, and most important of all, for the passenger, there were new ceiling panels, neat little bell pushes instead of the old ones which one struck with one's fist rather like attempting to wallop the bell on a fairground try-your-strength machine, chromium-plated hand and grab rails, linoleum instead of wooden slatted floors, and new upholstered seats upstairs. The result was a very neat looking car and it was only a pity that more could not have been so treated.

It was not the motorbus which replaced the tram throughout the 1930s, but the trolleybus. It might well have been that LT, if it had been starting from scratch, would have gone straight over to the diesel bus and there is evidence to suggest that it regarded the trolleybus only as an intermediate stage. However it wasn't starting from scratch, and although many of the tramcars and their tracks were worn out, the electrical equipment and infrastructure wasn't and could be used by the trolleys.

The first tram replacement scheme took place on 27 October 1935 when further former London United routes (many had already gone in 1931) in west London were replaced by trolleybus routes 657 Hounslow — Shepherd's Bush, and 667 Hampton Court — Hammersmith. Shortly afterwards, across the other side of London, on Sunday 10 November route 698 began operating between Bexleyheath and Woolwich, followed 14 days later by the 696 from Woolwich to Dartford. The vehicles, operating from a brand new depot at Bexleyheath, were chiefly short-wheelbase B2 class 60 seaters, although, as traffic increased, standard 70 seaters became the norm. The standard London trolleybus, closely based on No 62, the prototype of 1934, was a classic design, elegant and comfortable, and ahead of its time in many respects so that it never really looked dated, even when more than 20 years old. It did not, surprisingly, bear much resemblance to the current standard

Left:
A pair of ex-London United solid-tyred tower wagons at work on trolleybus overhead. *Topical*

Below:
Metropolitan clerestory-roofed B stock of 1905 and 1913 elliptical roof stock at Wembley Park station. To the far right is the big dipper of the Wembley Exhibition. *IAL*

Right:
One of the experimental streamlined tube two-car sets of 1935. *LT*

Below right:
R2, a Reliance rebodied in June 1935 with a Weymann body, a kind of single-deck equivalent of the STL. *IAL*

motorbus, the STL, not even in matters of livery — beyond a basic red — and route indicators, a reflection that the trolleybus department of LT was under the control of ex-tramway men who had their own ideas and were allowed to pursue them. Trams continued to operate as far as Abbey Wood and trams and trolleybuses ran side by side, for part of the way sharing the same wiring. A unique feature of this stage was the part replacement of the trams by a Country Area green bus route, 480.

Before the year was out a third tram replacement scheme was completed. On 8 December more 60-seater trolleys began working roughly half way between the two previous schemes, from West Croydon to Sutton Green, the 654 replacing South MET route 7.

Production of new single-deck buses to replace the motley collection inherited by the Country Area got under way during 1935. The main batch of Leyland Cubs, C2-75, began to enter service in the spring. At

the same time 100 full size single-deckers arrived from the AEC works at Southall. This surprised nobody, but much less expected was the fact that they were fitted with bodies by the Birmingham Railway Carriage and Wagon Co: truly remarkable was their layout, for they were side-engined Qs. This was far and away the biggest order AEC had received for the type. The body seated 37 passengers, soon reduced to 35 when the seats beside the driver's cab were removed to aid visibility. Although incorporating many standard LPTB features, there was a slight slope along the roofline from front to back. Designated 4Q4 they served London well and despite being of such an experimental nature, I remember them still working from Reigate and Dorking garages well after the war in the early 1950s.

The half-cab body for a forward control chassis also appeared in 1935, but none of the 43 new Weymann bodies went on new chassis. Twelve went on early AEC Regals, to be used briefly as Green Line coaches, while the remaining 31 went on even older, and outdated, AEC Reliance buses.

The Country Area continued to set the pace as far as innovation was concerned and its first standard STLs, Nos 959–1043 and 1056–9, which went into service from February 1935, had front entrances. In this they were following on from the lowbridge Godstone STLs, and elsewhere, Midland Red for example, front-entrance double-deckers were in production. Nevertheless the open rear platform was vastly more common and would remain so until rear engines and one-man operation came in some 25 years later. The thinking was that the front entrance, with a door, had proved successful in rural areas; unfortunately these standard STLs had no door, the Chiswick engineers claiming that they had nevertheless designed a draught free layout. Experience soon proved they hadn't. The front entrance STLs, coded 10STL6, seated only 48 passengers, the eight missing seats downstairs giving way to racks for luggage and parcels with which it was presumed the country folk of Romford, Slough, Sutton, et al, were usually encumbered, to say nothing of the straws behind their ears. A second batch of front-entrance STLs (1464-1513) began entering service in July 1936. Outwardly similar to the earlier ones, in fact they had Weymann metal-framed bodies. All 139 spent all their lives in the Country Area, working from numerous garages, so that they became a familiar sight on many routes for 15 years or more. Whenever we ventured out into the country from Croydon, I always tried to persuade my father to wait for one of these distinctive vehicles which operated from practically all of the many garages which sent green buses to Croydon. I don't think this included Godstone, which was rather curious given that it was the very first London Country garage to receive front-entrance double-deckers — the lowbridge Weymann version for the 410.

A curious one-off version of the STL appeared in November 1935. This was STL857. At that time, streamlining was all the rage — think of Gresley's 'A4' Pacifics built that year to haul the 'Silver Jubilee' — so STL857 had a full front, an ornamental grille concealing the radiator, and a rakishly inclined profile. It was renumbered into a class of its own, STF, at the end of the year, but remained unique and unloved, and was soon rebuilt, in 1938, with a standard STL half cab and normal radiator. Transferred to the chassis of STL1167 in 1939, the body was scrapped in 1950.

A feature we all take for granted as having been around as long as the bus itself is the fixed stop. In fact before the days of the LPTB a London bus would stop anywhere along its route if requested, just like a taxi. Trams and trolleys had always had fixed stops but the practice was only extended to the buses in 1935, initially between Euston Road and Seven Sisters, Tottenham, and soon to central London; the familiar stop, whether request or compulsory, has scarcely changed since.

On the Underground a series of experimental tube trains were put into service on the Piccadilly Line and extensively tested before orders for the production units were placed. The biggest step forward was in the mounting of all equipment below the floor. Advanced technology made this possible, allowing some 15 per cent increase in passenger capacity. Four six-car trains were built, three of them with streamlined fronts, giving them a startling appearance, which nowadays seems to have a very art deco feel about it. The fourth train had a flat front, with curved roof ends. This proved to be

rather more practical as there was after all little need for streamlining on a train which seldom reached a speed in excess of 35mph and that mostly in a tunnel!

New stock was also built for the surface lines, although this was essentially a repeat of an existing design, the L stock of 1932. Designated M class, there were 14 motor cars and 14 trailers from the Birmingham Railway Carriage & Wagon Co, and 26 trailers from another Birmingham firm, Metro-Cammell. The most remarkable feature of the M stock was that it was fitted with clerestory roofs. In this it may be said to have done no more than followed Underground traditions but for all that this was pretty remarkable. One thinks of the clerestory as being an essentially late Victorian and Edwardian feature and the Underground carriages of 1935 were the very last British standard gauge vehicles to be fitted with them.

The rebuilding of Leicester Square station was completed in 1935 with a circular booking hall and what was claimed to be the longest escalator in the world serving the Piccadilly Line.

1936

The replacement of London's trams proceeded apace in 1936, both north and south of the river, east and west of the City and the West End. First, on 9 February the 654 trolleybus route was extended from Croydon, past Crystal Palace's football ground, through Anerley and up the steep hill to Crystal Palace itself, the fierce 1 in 9 necessitating the fitting of run-back brakes to the B1 trolleys, Nos 64-93,

which operated the route out of Sutton depot. The period when the famous Crystal Palace was served by trolleybuses lasted only a matter of months for, on the night of 30 November 1936, it burned down. Crowds came from all over London to watch the spectacle, although, truth to tell, they hardly needed to for the glow from Norwood Heights was visible for many miles around. Despite the many, many such fires which were to rage during the Blitz, the night the Crystal Palace burned down is still spoken of, not only by those elderly local inhabitants who can remember it, but by later generations to whom the spectacle has been recounted. Indeed when I taught at a secondary school in South Norwood in the late 1960s black pupils who had been born in the Caribbean knew all about the great burning of the Crystal Palace more than 30 years earlier. During the fire, and for some time afterwards, the 654s had to turn round at the bottom of the hill in Penge.

The next tram replacement was the ex-LUT route 89 from Hammersmith to Acton which became the trolleybus route 660 on 5 April. Curiously this lasted only until 5 July when it and former MET tram routes 66 and 68 which linked Acton and Canons Park were replaced by trolleybus route 666 which ran from Hammersmith to Edgware via Acton, Harlesden and Cricklewood. However the 660 reappeared later that summer on 2 August, this time running between Hammersmith and North Finchley. The 645 from Edgware to North Finchley was also introduced, ex-MET tram routes 45 and 60 disappearing. A number of the C class trolleys allocated these routes from Stonebridge depot had distinctive spats fitted over their rear wheels, a unique feature on a London trolleybus. Before August was out yet another section of the one-time MET network serving northwest London had gone, the 62 and 64s being replaced by 662 from Paddington Green to Sudbury and 664 Paddington Green to Edgware.

Next to go was a former LCC route in the northeast suburbs; the 73 which ran from the Royal Albert Docks to Wanstead Park. There was no direct replacement, the 101 bus, which covered most of the route, being strengthened. Staying in that part of London the 23 tram route was replaced on 18 October by the 623 trolleybus which ran from Woodford, Napier Arms to Manor House.

On 15 November the most westerly point in London reached by trams saw them no more when route 7 from Shepherd's Bush Green was replaced by the 607

trolleybus. Finally for 1936 the companion 655 trolleybus route came into operation on 13 December, replacing tram 55 and running between Hammersmith and Hanwell, being extended to Acton during weekday rush hours. The 7 had been worked by London's most modern trams, the Felthams. Unlike the other ex-LUT cars these were far too good to scrap and so they were sent south of the river to Telford Avenue which was the only depot with sufficient clearance to accommodate them.

The loss suffered by the citizens of west London was a gain for southerners. Stanley Collins, a driver at Telford Avenue, in his biography *The Wheels used to talk to us* (Tallis Publishing, 1977) writes: 'We thought they were fine, just loved to get out and drive one of them . . . I can't praise them too much . . . At first the passengers used to let the Standards go by

Above:
Former MET A type bogie tram No 2460 working route 66 shortly before withdrawal. *Author's collection*

Left:
Leaning back STL484 of Chalk Farm garage stands at the terminus of route 3 beside the Crystal Place shortly before it was burnt down.

Right:
Feltham No 2190 in typical southside territory working the 10 from Southwark to Tooting Broadway. *IAL*

just so that they could ride on a Feltham.' They did indeed, for I had the good luck to travel to school every day on Feltham routes 16 or 18, and I would always wait for one if I had the time. I don't think I've ever cared quite as much for any public transport vehicle as I did for the Felthams. They ran beautifully, cruising for long distances with the power off, putting every other type of tram to shame, and never rattled like buses did. Their fame spread far and wide and I once had a discussion on their merits in the Paris Transport Museum with a Frenchman who remembered them with affection. I am sure they will be there in spirit when the trams run once again in Croydon, their ghosts triumphant.

What many consider the truly classic and most handsome version of the STL appeared in October 1936. This was the 'roof number box bus'. All the remaining standard STLs, 360 in all, would be built to this design. Its fame spread far beyond London for Dinky Toys chose it as the basis for the first reasonably accurate mass produced model bus and even today no swap meet or decent model shop is without several, sometimes dozens, on offer. Indeed I bought one of the early postwar ones, in need of repainting but otherwise undamaged, last Saturday, for £9, which is roughly equivalent to what it would have cost when new. The first of the batch finished off the CXX registration numbers, then came DGX and DLU and it is the latter which is perhaps most associated with these buses, for most of the last survivors belonged to this group.

Single-deckers continued to arrive in large numbers during 1936. A most interesting class was the Inter-Station Cubs, strictly speaking one-and-a-half-deckers. Eight were built to work between the main line stations and they were given very large luggage lockers at the rear with a raised seating section above. They were painted in a delightful blue and yellow livery with black roofs and were numbered C106-113. The revolutionary Q class continued to find far more favour in London than elsewhere and two further

Above:
Yours for a penny, Green Line Q195.

versions entered service in 1936. Q106–185, coded 5Q5, were designed as 37-seat buses, 53 for the Central Area, the remaining 27 for the Country Area. They were the only ones to have an entrance forward of the front wheels, level with the driver, and might easily have been used as OMO buses had they been a generation later. Fitted with Park Royal bodies they were probably the best looking of the London Qs, anticipating features perpetuated in the RT, and still looked modern when they were replaced by the RF class in 1952-3.

Q189–238, coded 6Q6, were 32-seat coaches, also with Park Royal bodies. The entrance, with its

sliding door, returned to a position behind the front wheels. Because of the underfloor engine there had to be longitudinal seats over the front wheel arches for six passengers in all, not ideal for a coach, but they nevertheless worked hard. Many went to Hertford and Guildford garages, returning there after the war.

1936 saw the first appearance of a completely new, conventional single-decker. Fifty Regals with Weymann 30-seat bodies, T403-452 went into Green Line service. Coded 9T9 they had a rather curious frontal appearance in that a gaiter, or collar, surrounded the radiator, the nearside headlamp was built into the bonnet and a bumper completed the somewhat clumsy effect. The rear four of the 30 seats were raised as were the two rearmost windows on each side.

1937

1937 saw a new double-deck class enter service, one which was to prove particularly popular with drivers, engineers and passengers. LT put in an order to Leyland for 100 Titan TD4s to be fitted with Leyland bodies. In order to make the bodies resemble the STL, one of this class was lent to the Lancashire firm and the result was a bus which looked very like the standard Chiswick product, although enthusiasts had great fun spotting the differences. The standard Leyland radiator was, of course, fitted and the class was designated STD. A roof number box layout was chosen and the registration numbers were DLU 311–410. The final 10 were originally fitted with torque converters but these reverted to a standard clutch and gearbox in 1939. Sent to Hendon garage

the STDs were a familiar sight on the 13 and the 113 and consequently frequently featured in pictures of Oxford Street in the period 1937–52.

A very different Leyland put into service in December was TF1. This was a 34-seat coach with an underfloor engine and a cab of quite extraordinary aspect. In theory there was no need to retain the half-cab layout — it had been abandoned in the Q class — but as the front wheels were in a conventional position instead of being set back, it was.

In February the last, and least successful, of the Q class, was taken into stock. Q188 looked splendid, being a six-wheel Park Royal-bodied double-deck coach, but it was underpowered and, so it is said, met with trade union opposition. In the event it never ran in Green Line service and did not carry passengers until the following year. It then did a brief, two-year stint as a Country Area bus before being withdrawn at the outbreak of war. It never worked again in LT service, being sold in 1946 for service along the shores of the Clyde west of Glasgow where it seems to have found the climate much to its liking.

In complete contrast was the Underground stock which entered service on the District and Metropolitan lines in 1937. Although now all withdrawn, these trains were for decades, along with the tube stock introduced the following year, the epitome of modern travel below the streets of London and were, like the standard trolleybus, the STL and the 10T10 Green Line coach, a classic design which put LT in the very forefront of urban transport worldwide. They were known as the Metadyne, on account of a new system of control pioneered by Metropolitan Vickers and tried out in 1934, or O and P stock. In all the 573 carriages, which included 205 Q stock, introduced in 1938 to work with older vehicles, had transformed the Underground system by the time the last entered

Above left:
Inter-station Cub C108 and a lady in a hurry meet at Victoria.

Left:
A scene in Chiswick High Road with B3 class trolleybus No 473 on the 655, whilst a shortly-to-be-withdrawn Green Line Leyland Tiger overtakes STL1805 heading for Highgate. *LT*

Right:
One of a fleet of 25 luxury coaches being built at Addlestone . . . when finished these will be the very latest in luxury travel and five of them will be fitted with wireless which will 'pick up the world'. An LTC under construction. *Topical*

Left:
Metropolitan Railway 4-4-4T at Chorley Wood with the down Pullman express for Verney Junction.
Real Photos

Left:
Maunsell-designed former Metropolitan Railway 2-6-4T passing Chorley Wood with a down passenger train. *Real Photos*

Below:
A Richmond-bound District Line train of Q stock approaching Kew Gardens. *C. C. B. Herbert*

Above:
A brand new STD12. *LT*

service in 1941. They looked very different to anything which had gone before, being completely flush-sided, the windows using rebated glass. The lower panels were flared outwards, a feature said to have been devised to prevent would-be passengers clinging to the outside after the automatic doors had been closed. It has never been deemed necessary for later stock to be so equipped and one wonders whether it wasn't simply there for stylistic reasons. Whatever, it resulted in a highly distinctive carriage. Tried out between High Street Kensington and Putney Bridge from September 1937, the O stock began work on the Hammersmith and City line in December.

Meanwhile work was proceeding on extending the system and building, or rebuilding, many stations, all showing LT's concern with aesthetics, with the result that a number of them are now listed buildings. In central London, Earls Court was rebuilt to cater for the new exhibition hall; the previous year Eastcote, on the Metropolitan Line, had been given a new station built into an accompanying row of streets, all to the

same style. The extensions to the Central, Northern and Bakerloo lines were all going ahead. Acton Central Overhaul Shops was rebuilt, its capacity raised from 3,000 to 5,000 cars. Neasden running sheds were also rebuilt and one spin-off from this was the transfer of LT's largest and most modern steam engines, chiefly used to haul passenger trains beyond Rickmansworth, to the LNER. These included the four G class 0-6-4Ts, the eight H class 4-4-4Ts and the six K class 2-6-4Ts. All inherited from the Metropolitan Railway, they were a particularly fine looking group of locomotives. Their subsequent careers were short and ignominious, ending far away from their old home.

New locomotives which entered service in 1937 were LT's first battery ones. Constructed from redundant tube cars, these service vehicles were 55ft long, weighed 56 tons, had a maximum speed of 30mph and were designed to run off either the live rail or from their banks of accumulators.

Heavy inroads were made into the tram systems of east London and elsewhere in 1937. First to go, in January, was the 85, a former Walthamstow Corporation route, which was replaced by the 685. This trolleybus route was extended over the years and eventually ran from the Crooked Billet in

Walthamstow to Silvertown, with some peak hour journeys even reaching the river at North Woolwich. There was a wait of nearly six months before a whole collection of Docklands trams were replaced in June, the 69, 87, 97, 97A, 99 and 99A, all disappearing, while the 55 and 57 were cut back. Stratford Broadway, one of the busiest tram meeting places, now became equally popular with the trolleybus. The 669 ran to Canning Town, while the 687, 697 and 699 (the highest number of all London's trolleybus routes) all connected Chingford Mount and the Victoria and Albert Docks, by various routes.

Over in West London, in September, the 32 from Clapham Common to Chelsea Bridge was replaced by an existing bus route, the revised 137, while four days later, on 12 September, a much more extensive replacement saw a further Croydon tram route, the 30, disappear, to be replaced by one of London's longest trolleybus routes, the 630, which extended just over 14 miles from West Croydon to the quirkily named 'Near Willesden Junction'. The rest of this stage consisted of cutbacks rather than complete withdrawals. The 12 tram route now operated between Wandsworth and London Bridge; a new trolleybus route, 612, served Battersea and Mitcham; the 6 was cut back from Mitcham to run between Tooting and Southwark; the 14 and 31 ceased to run between Battersea and Wandsworth; and the 26 and 28 were seen no more west of Clapham Junction, safe from Red Indian ambush. New trolleybus routes were the rush-hour-only 626 Clapham Junction-Acton and the 628 Clapham Junction-Harlesden; Craven Park. Wandsworth depot now operated both trolleybus and trams and would continue to do so until October 1950.

On the same day, 12 September, one of the two London No 1 tram routes disappeared, along with 1A, linking Stratford with East Ham and Upton Park respectively. Almost at the other numerical end, routes 95 (Wanstead Flats-Canning Town) and 95A (Wanstead Flats-Upton Park) were also withdrawn, all these being replaced by an extension of the 685 trolleybus route to Canning Town and a new Stratford Circular, 689. After only a few months anti-clockwise, 689s were renumbered 690.

On the single-deck bus (or rather coach) front the year ended with a surprising new class, a petrol-engined six-wheeler. This was the LTC, comprising 24 very imposing looking Weymann-bodied private hire vehicles. Curiously they were slightly shorter than the 9T9s. Both petrol engines, reconditioned Mk 1 Comets removed from LTs, and the four-wheel bogie, virtually identical to that used on the trolleybuses, were said to have been chosen to give the smoothest possible ride.

Below:
The caption for this Keystone picture taken on 5 August 1937 reads 'Poor kiddies left Canning Town this morning for a day's outing in coaches (sic) as the guests of the Transport Workers' Children's Outing Fund.'

Yet another variation of the STL completes our look at 1937. The only Thames road crossings downriver from Tower Bridge, apart from the Woolwich Free Ferry, were the Blackwall and Rotherhithe tunnels. Neither had been designed with the heavy motor traffic of the 1930s in mind and there was limited clearance, particularly at Blackwall. Specially modified NSs, mostly still with solid tyres, operated the tunnel routes, and they were now past their sell-by date. So 40 new STLs, with reinforced tyres, heavily domed roofs and tapered rear ends entered service in March and April. By 1938 all were concentrated at Athol Street garage, Poplar, where they stayed for the rest of their careers. Because of the roof modifications the number indicator at the front reverted to a position between the decks. 1937 was the last year of the NS in passenger service, as it was of the numerically very small LS class of six-wheelers, immediate predecessor of the LT. The last NS, No 1974, came out of service on 30 November. Both NS and LS with their high clearance, squat radiators and various other features, by this date looked archaic. However a number of the NSs survived as staff canteens until the early 1950s. I remember one, No 2295, serving at Chelsham garage alongside brand new RTs; how I wish I had started taking photographs back then. Four LSs became breakdown tenders and these lasted until 1951. One NS, No 1995, was preserved by LT, and I *did* get a picture of this when it first went on display at the Museum of British Transport at

Clapham in the late 1960s in exactly the condition it was in when taken out of service on the 29, and before it was spruced up and repainted.

1938

The last full year of peace was perhaps LT's finest, when it was innovating at full throttle, sweeping away trams with smooth, silent trolleybuses, modernising both surface and tube railway lines with fleets of the most up-to-date trains. By this time the hotchpotch of vehicles it had inherited for its Green Line services had almost entirely given way to a series of handsome, comfortable new coaches. Also in 1938, although the STL was still in full production and still being refined, there appeared the first of its successors — a class which would eventually number 4825, with another 2,131 very similar Leyland buses.

The 1938 Tube stock would eventually number no less than 1,221 vehicles. Based on the flat-fronted experimental unit of 1935, the biggest innovation introduced with these trains was that all the electrical equipment and traction motors were beneath the floor,

Below:
Former MET H-class bogie car No 2217 of 1910-2 at the Bruce Grove terminus of route 19.

Left:
A bespatted C class trolleybus does its best to obscure the soon to be redundant tram lines at King's Cross. It is working route 517 North Finchley-Holborn introduced on 6 March 1938. STLs and LTs in the background. *LT*

Above:
1938 Tube stock.

allowing a significant increase in capacity. Like the surface stock of the previous year, the new tube trains presented a very smooth, albeit rather more conventional, outline. Metro-Cammell built 644 DM (Driving motor) cars and 107 NDM (non-driving motors) cars, while BRCW built the remaining 99 NDM cars and 271 trailer cars. They entered service on the Northern and Bakerloo lines, 58 of the 1927 trailers being converted to work with the 1938 stock on the latter. Because the LNER retained ownership of the track over which the Northern Line was extended to High Barnet and Mill Hill, some of the stock actually belonged to the company, although the only indication of this was a plate inscribed 'Property of the LNER' on the underframes. There would seem to be no record of it attempting to attach itself to a Gresley Pacific and hightailing for the Scottish border.

While on matters electrical the demise has to be recorded of 23 more tram routes and their replacement by 20 trolleybus and one motorbus ones. The biggest inroads were into the north London routes and for the first time a number of the LCC's standard tram, the E1, a class which exceeded 1,000, was taken out of service. Between 1926 and 1930, the year the final 50 of the class appeared, they had been modernised with upholstered seating and various other improvements, although the fitting of windscreens was not completed until 1940, many being withdrawn without them.

First to go, on 6 February, were two local Barking routes: 91 and 93, being replaced by the 691 from Barkingside to Barking Broadway and the 693 Chadwell Heath-Barking Broadway. There was also the 692 from Newbury Park to Chadwell Heath which ran on Saturdays, but not for long, disappearing the next year.

A minor withdrawal later that month was the 37 from Wood Green to Alexandra Palace, although it was of considerable historical interest in that it marked the end of single-deck tram operation in London — that is until the late 1990s! The 241A motorbus route replaced it at first, then a few months later an extension of the 233. There were plans to incorporate the LNER's Alexandra Palace branch into the Underground network but these never

Left:
Green Line T522.

Below:
Victoria in 1938 with almost as many
STLs, LTs and one STD as people,
with a leavening of taxis, one bicycle
and a Rolls-Royce.

materialised and the line eventually faded away after the war. Alexandra Palace, in many ways north London's answer to Crystal Palace, set up on the heights above Wood Green and the LNER line out of King's Cross, was at this time home to the world's first regular TV service and when its 50th anniversary was celebrated in 1986 in a delightfully nostalgic Jack Rosenthal documentary drama, the one and only preserved 10T10 Green Line coach played a starring role.

1938 saw the introduction of these fine vehicles, 266 of them. A modified version of the 9T9 with a larger engine, they possessed none of that breed's slight ungainliness. They became the vehicles which

everyone of my generation associated with the exalted standards of appearance and comfort which epitomised Green Line services in the late 1930s and 1940s. T453-602 originally seated 30 passengers, T603-718 seated 34. The AEC diesel engine was rated at 8.8 litres; the body was built by LT at Chiswick.

Yet another innovative single-decker entered service in January 1938. This was CR1, a Leyland Cub with a rear engine. Painted green it was sent to work at St Albans. In appearance there were similarities with TF1.

STLs, having replaced all the NSs, were now being used to oust the Central Area TD class, Leyland Titans absorbed in 1933 from various sources. By June 1938 production of STLs temporarily ceased, with no more appearing till the following year.

One TD body found further use for a short while, a use which gave it a permanent place in the history of the motorbus. The Dodson body of TD111 was put on to a brand new chassis and on 13 July 1938 the bus was taxed ready for use and given the fleet number ST1140. It was sent to Hanwell garage (later known as Southall) — the traditional home of experimental buses at this time — and took up work there. The

registration number was EYK 396 and it was, of course, the prototype RT.

Now back to the tram replacement programme. In March no less than nine routes disappeared, although one, the Sundays only 11X, was to be revived. Those permanently withdrawn were the 9, 13, 17, 19, 21, 35A, 39A and 51. The new trolleybus routes were the 517/617 and 521/621 North Finchley-Holborn Circus, 609 Barnet-Moorgate and the 651 Barnet-Golders Green and Cricklewood motorbus route 134 was strengthened. The conversion of Finchley depot meant that the MET Felthams were redundant and they travelled south to join their former LUT brothers at Telford Avenue.

May saw the end of tram routes 29, 39, 41 and 41EX, being replaced by the 625 Wood Green-Walthamstow, the 629 Enfield-Tottenham Court Road and the 641 Winchmore Hill-Moorgate. Next, in July, the 3, 5, 7 and 15 disappeared, the 513/613 Hampstead Heath-Holborn Circus, the 615 Parliament Hill Fields-Moorgate and the 639 Hampstead Heath-Moorgate taking over.

In October trams disappeared from their northernmost London outpost, Waltham Cross, the 59 and 79 being replaced by the 659 from Waltham Cross to Holborn Circus and the 679 from Waltham Cross (Sundays only) and Ponders End (weekdays) to Smithfield. The 679 soon saw a good deal more of Waltham Cross, being extended there on Monday to Friday rush hours and all day on Saturdays at the next tram replacement in November. This saw the end of the 27 and the 49A, while the 49 was cut back. New routes were the 627 Tottenham Court Road-Edmonton and the 649 Stamford Hill-Ponders End.

1939

We noted the appearance of the first RT, heavily disguised, in 1938, but it was in April 1939 when the complete bus, with its new body, was eventually finished. As befitted such a landmark it was inspected and modified in several matters, notably livery, before it was officially shown to the press on 13 July. Happily RT1 still exists, at least the body does — the

chassis being a postwar one — and is often seen at rallies, so its appearance will be familiar to many and there is no need to describe it in detail. But it must be said that both internally and externally new heights had been reached and there are those who think they have never since been excelled. Here and there one could see a family likeness to the latest STLs, but there was much that was different, the four bay windows, the lower radiator, the superb interior where the minutest attention had been paid to every detail. Probably the feature which most appealed to LPTB drivers was the sliding cab door. In July RT1 was sent to Chelverton Road garage, Putney and on Wednesday 9 August it entered passenger service, on the 22 from Putney Common to Homerton.

The arrival of RT1 did not immediately signal the end of the STL because what was intended to be a final batch, Nos 2516–2647, had been ordered the previous year, STL2647 entering service in September 1939 from Alperton garage. Given FJJ and FXT registration marks, they were instantly recognisable from previous batches by their longer radiators and wheel discs. There were improvements to the chassis and there was a direct injection engine which resulted in improved fuel consumption and easier starting. For the first time standard rear entrance STLs went direct into Country Area service: 39 were painted green and sent southeastwards to Northfleet and Dartford. The

arrival of these STLs meant the end of the oil-engined TD class in both Central and Country areas and, more significantly, the first withdrawals of the Tilling STs. By this date the oldest of these buses was into its 10th year, about the average life of their predecessors, the NS class, and had not the war intervened, many more STs and LTs would no doubt have been earmarked for early withdrawal.

The two unorthodox, experimental single-deckers of 1937-8, the TF and CR, were both considered to have justified production orders from Leyland and so TF2-88 and CR2-49 arrived during 1939. TF2-13 were touring coaches with a generous allocation of curved glass in the canted roof panels and a sliding central section, while the remainder went into Green Line service from Luton, St Albans, Grays and Dorking, enabling the last of the pre-1933 petrol-engined Ts to be demoted to buses. Both had conventional cabs, a design to which TF1 was altered. The CR class, Nos 2–49, were also somewhat different in appearance to the prototype, these having straight sides instead of a stepped waistline. By the time they had arrived so had the war and, although they went into limited service, they were not trouble free and by 1941 all were in store.

Production of trolleybuses by both Leyland and AEC continued apace and was unaffected by the outbreak of war. Three new routes appeared in February, the 643 Wood Green-Holborn Circus, the 647 Stamford Hill-London Docks and the 683 Stamford Hill-Moorgate, while the 649 was extended from Stamford Hill to Liverpool Street. Tram routes 43, 47, 49, 49EX, 71, 75 and 83 disappeared. A month later the 53 was replaced by the 653 which ran in a big loop from Tottenham Court Road to Aldgate via Stamford Hill.

In June most of the tram routes serving Leyton and the approaches to Epping Forest, the 55, 55EX, 57, 57EX, 81 and 81EX disappeared, and the 31 was cut back from the Bakers Arms to Hackney. The trolley replacements were the 555 Bloomsbury-Leyton Green and Downsell Road, the 557 Liverpool Street-Chingford Mount and the 581 Bloomsbury-Woodford (Napier Arms). The 687 was withdrawn between Leyton and Chingford Mount. A week after the outbreak of war the 77 was withdrawn and replaced by the 677 from West India Docks to Smithfield, while on Guy Fawkes' Day, which was certainly not celebrated, the 61 and 63 were replaced by the 661 from Aldgate to the Bakers Arms, Leyton and the 663 from Aldgate to Ilford. Finally on 10 December the 11 and 11EX were replaced by the 611 Highgate Village to Moorgate and the Sundays only 611EX Highgate Village-Islington Green. There was just one more replacement programme to go.

On the Underground the New Works Programme continued unabated. The Bakerloo Line reached

Left:
Former LCC E1 class tram No 1188, dating from 1908-9 and still without windscreens, heading for Smithfield on service 77. Both tram and route were withdrawn on 10 September 1939. *Author's collection*

Right:
Brand new STL2569, delivered to Hanwell Garage in March 1939, at London Bridge. *G. Robbins collection*

Stanmore and on 20 November the revised services, relieving the bottleneck north of Baker Street, began. Surfacing near Finchley Road, the Bakerloo tube trains operated an all-stations service to Wembley Park, while the Metropolitan ones, on separate tracks, ran non-stop to Wembley Park. In July the Northern Line reached East Finchley, taking over former LNER tracks, the 17-mile long tunnel from there to Morden, via the Bank, being at that time the longest in the world. Work was also completed on rebuilding stations in central London on the Piccadilly and Central lines, while the conversion of the Great Northern and City Line from the two current rails being outside the running ones to standard configuration was carried out.

From the foregoing it might seem the outbreak of war had little immediate effect on LT. This is quite untrue. Even before war was declared many buses were on war work carrying service personnel and others to their posts; all Green Line services ceased on Friday 1 September, the Tube lines under the Thames were temporarily closed and bus services substituted, and vast numbers of children were evacuated, taken by bus, tram and trolleybus to the stations where the main line trains were waiting for them.

Left:
Green Line passengers, September 1939.

Below:
RT1, as restored in 1979, its body mounted on a postwar chassis.

Above:
TF9 in all its original glory, poses for its official portrait on 17 April 1939. By a quirk of fate this was the only one of the sightseeing TFs away from Bull Yard, Peckham when a bomb destroyed all the others.

Yet normal life continued. Almost my earliest memory is of being taken by my parents on Sunday 3 September 1939, the day war was declared, for an outing by the river at Richmond. I was two years and two months old. We had travelled there by tram and Southern Railway electric train. It was a gloriously sunny day and I can remember waiting for the train home on Richmond station when the air raid sirens sounded. Most people expected instant aerial attack and terrible devastation and something of the panic must have conveyed itself to me, although I doubt if it came from my parents. My father had served throughout World War 1 as a driver in the Middle East; my mother's father had been killed at Gallipoli. Anyhow nothing happened, the train duly appeared and we eventually arrived home safely. Only last year, while visiting the local museum in Richmond the volunteer attendant, a native of the town who remembered the incident well, provided the sequel to the story. The sirens sounded because radar had picked up an aircraft approaching across the English Channel which seemed to be heading straight for the Richmond area. It transpired it was a British aeroplane coming back from France to the Vickers Works at Weybridge but such was the understandable nervousness that the alarm was sounded when it couldn't be identified instantly.

The blackout was imposed immediately, headlamps were masked and interior lights dimmed. This caused many problems and a number of accidents, and one attempt to alleviate some of the dangers was the painting of front mudguard edges in white, with a large white spot on the rear of motorbuses. Trolleybuses did not have the spot so that they could be distinguished and other trolleybus drivers would not attempt to overtake them. Trams had their fenders painted white.

Apart from the withdrawal of Green Line services — there was a temporary, partial restoration a little later — there were many service cuts right across LT and a number of smaller capacity vehicles were withdrawn, ranging from Dennis Darts to STs and front entrance STLs. The entire fleet of Tilling STs was taken out of service.

1940

For almost a year after the declaration of war the threatened aerial bombardment of London failed to materialise; the fall of France and the Dunkirk evacuation in June 1940 brought the Phoney War to an end. The first damage inflicted by enemy aircraft was on trolleybus wires at New Malden on 16 August. Initially, and perhaps rather unexpectedly, it was the rural and suburban areas south of the Thames which suffered, chiefly those near strategic targets, such as the Vickers aircraft factory at Weybridge which was badly damaged on 4 September. The first bomb fell on the City of London on 24 August and by the end of the month the Blitz on both suburbs and central London, particularly Docklands and the East End, north and south of the river, was at its height. The disruption and damage was immense. Tram and trolleybus services were particularly vulnerable, their tracks and wires being destroyed; often they could be diverted, but bus services suffered too. Nevertheless temporary tracks and overhead wiring were often set up in a very short time. Many vehicles were destroyed, and although in a number of instances crew and passengers were able to take shelter before a raid began, they weren't always so lucky and there were a number of deaths and a great many injuries. Vehicles were patched up and boarded-up windows became a common sight. Anti-blast netting, first with a small rectangle, later a little diamond left clear in the centre, was stuck on windows. With the perversity typical of people living in extreme conditions who nevertheless try to treat life as normally as possible, I

can remember how we complained about the inconvenience this caused, particularly the nasty yellow colour the glass turned, and we would always try, if possible, to sit beside a window which had not been so treated.

In some respects the damage to buses, trams, trolleys and trains was less than might have been expected, given the overall intensity of the Blitz, and seeing what happened to German cities in the later years of the war. But it has to be remembered that most of the raids took place at night; each evening the sirens would wail, I would be roused from my bed by my mother and we would sit under the stairs — my father would be out performing his warden duties — we would only use the Anderson shelter at the bottom of the garden if the raid seemed to be particularly intense and aimed at us personally. Most public transport had ceased to run and was off the streets and in garages and depots or dispersed in various locations. If bombs fell directly on these locations then of course vehicles were destroyed and it was here that most of the casualties took place.

It would take several pages to list all the damage to parked vehicles, but in the latter part of 1940 mention must be made of 10 Tilling STs written off at Leyton garage, 30 trams at Camberwell depot, four buses at Camberwell garage, eight trams at Abbey Wood, six at New Cross, 16 at Clapham and 53 buses and coaches at the former Thomas Tilling depot at Peckham. No less than 11 of the grand total of 12 of the virtually new TF touring coaches, Nos 2–8 and 10–13, were lost here, leaving TF9 — which was elsewhere — as the sole survivor for the next 12 years. There were many other examples of bodies being damaged beyond repair but the chassis surviving. The one trolleybus depot to suffer serious damage at this time, Bexleyheath, lost four trolleybus bodies but their chassis received new bodies from Weymann. Given that so many trolleybuses operated in East London, it was remarkable that they suffered much less than the motorbus and tram fleets.

Londoners took to tube stations at night to escape the bombing, unofficially and often chaotically at first, but soon on an organised basis. The Central Line tunnels beyond Liverpool Street, completed but not yet operational, were lived in day and night in some cases. However complete safety was not guaranteed even underground. On 14 October a bomb penetrated the Northern Line station at Balham, exploded and 68 people died. The line was not reopened for three months. There were other deaths on the tube but the District, Metropolitan and Circle lines were much more vulnerable, the worst incident being at Sloane Square station on 12 November when there were many deaths. I never used to pass through it, on our way to regular outings at South Kensington, without a shiver of apprehension.

Apart from war damage the fleet underwent a number of changes, not the least being that new vehicles continued to be delivered. The Green Line fleet of modern coaches, some 477 vehicles, had been converted in 1939 into ambulances. However some coaches had been released before the end of 1939 and took up Green Line service again. The Blitz brought about a reorganisation; cross-London services ceased, but nevertheless 33 routes were operating at the end of the year.

The final conversion to trolleybuses took part when the last east London trams disappeared on 9 June. Routes 65, 65EX, 67 and 67EX were replaced by the 565 Holborn Circus-East Ham, the 567, which led a

Below:
A scene at Golders Green in May 1940, a few weeks before the Blitz hit London. A 10T10 Green Line coach with white lines marking its passenger entrance passes two STLs, a former LGOC Central Area T stands in the station forecourt, a train of 1938 Tube stock crosses the bridge while two trolleybuses pass beneath it. *LT*

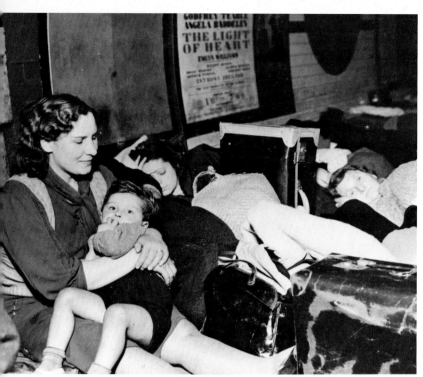

Below:
The caption of this Fox Photo dated 12 September 1940, reads: 'This omnibus in South London was blown to pieces when hit by a bomb during yesterday evening's raid over London.' Hopefully the passengers and crew had reached the shelter on the opposite pavement in time. The route details of the damaged Tilling STL further up the road have been scratched out by the censor.

Right:
STL1988 negotiates a temporary crossing over a bomb crater, 7 December 1940. *Fox*

very complicated life style, running between Aldgate and West Ham Mondays to Fridays, Aldgate to Barking Broadway on Saturdays, and Smithfield to Poplar on Sundays, and finally the 665 Bloomsbury to Barking Broadway. Even after this new, trolleybuses continued to be delivered well into 1941. The only trams now seen north of the river, other than along the

Embankment, were the three Kingsway Subway routes — 31, 33, 35 — which penetrated some way into the northern suburbs, and the 34 which terminated at the unfashionable end of the King's Road, Chelsea.

Much the brightest spot in this chapter of many horrors was the arrival of the first production RTs, the first seven entering service from Chelverton Road,

Putney, on 2 January. Although generally referred to as the 'prewar RTs', this of course really only applies to RT1, but nevertheless they were built totally to prewar standards. Officially coded RT2, they were superficially very little different to RT1. 338 had been ordered, but clearly this was too optimistic under wartime conditions and production stopped with the delivery of the 150th chassis to Chiswick in May. The building of the bodies took much longer and many RTs were still waiting completion at the end of the year. Some of the later ones went to a new garage, opened on   20 March 1940. This was Gillingham Street (GM), situated just behind Victoria station and close to the elegant squares which typify the area south of Buckingham Palace Road. As the only garage in the West End it inevitably became one of the best known and was home over the years to many vehicles of especial distinction.

Frank Pick retired from LT in 1940. As chief executive from its creation he had headed what was described at the time as 'the world's finest integrated urban transport system' and in an article in the *Independent* newspaper in March 1995, Jonathan Glancey called him 'the greatest patron of the arts in Britain this century.' This remarkable man was well paid for his extraordinary achievements, £10,000 a year, 43 times that of a London bus driver who, as Jonathan Glancey pointed out, was 'among the best-paid workers in Britain'. The latter is a claim no one would make about a London bus driver in 1995.

1941

The Blitz continued unabated through the early months of 1941. Bank station was hit on 11 January and the road above it collapsed, causing traffic chaos for weeks. West Ham depot, newly converted from tram to trolleybus, was damaged in March and L2 class trolleybus No 1492 was destroyed, the only such occurrence during the Blitz. Croydon garage suffered terrible devastation, the worst in the entire LT area. The raid took place on Saturday 10 May and, ironically, it almost marked the end of the Blitz. Four staff were killed and 58 buses destroyed. Croydon, being an ex-Tilling garage, possessed an elderly fleet of petrol-engined vehicles mainly of Tilling and London General origin, but nevertheless LT could ill afford to lose them. I used to be slightly miffed that we had to make do with such antiques and I would have been perfectly happy if something rather more modern had been drafted in. No such luck, there was a whip round and by Monday morning some 50 odd General and Tilling STs from all over London had filled the breach. The former continued to provide the

Below:
A Bluebird LT negotiates the temporary bridge over the emergency staircases being erected at the bombed Bank station, 15 March 1941. *LT*

bulk of Croydon's allocation until the RT era. One particular memory I have of a journey in a 60-seat General STL on the 59B heading home from Coulsdon is of a rumour spreading through the bus as we approached Purley that the police were stopping all traffic to check identity cards; it was obvious from the agitation of my parents and a number of other passengers in the crowded bus that they hadn't got them. I can't recall precisely what happened next but we kept our seats and arrived home safely.

A curious episode occurred during the Blitz when an appeal went out for buses to be sent from the provinces to help out in London. It was curious because, given the size of London's fleet, relatively few vehicles had actually been written off, and service reductions meant that a considerable number of perfectly usable vehicles, both buses and trams, were actually in store. Perhaps it was the crews who were needed, perhaps it was all a publicity stunt to show that Britain was united in the war effort and would not let the capital down. In the event a wonderfully kaleidoscopic variety of liveries brightened up the sombre, war-torn streets. 475 buses, mostly double-deckers but some single, came from all over Scotland, Wales and England, plus 18 bright yellow trolleybuses from Bournemouth. The first, an orange, green and cream Regent from Halifax, arrived on 22 October. Some did not stay long and all had gone home by February 1942, except for two Manchester

Corporation Crossleys destroyed in the Croydon garage bombing.

Towards the end of 1941 the process was reversed when five Tilling STs were sent to help devastated Coventry. These were the first of many, 291 in all, which left London to help out in the provinces. They were all STs of various types. Some stayed much longer than any provincial bus did in London, the very last not returning until 1948 — when they were immediately sent to the scrapyard!

As if to compound the oddness of the influx of buses from far and wide, delivery continued not only of RTs and trolleybuses, but also resumed of STLs and STDs. Production of the standard 'prewar' trolleybus finally ended in October when P1 class No 1721 entered service. From the B1s of 1935 to the final P1s would seem to encompass a great many classes: but this is misleading. Beyond the fact that some were Leylands and others AECs, there was scarcely little more variation than within the STL class. To quote S. L. Poole in the 1949 edition of *abc of London's Trams and Trolleybuses*: 'The London trolleybuses are of three types — (i) the standard vehicle seating 70, with the short wheelbase modification seating the lesser number as noted, (ii) the chassisless pattern introduced immediately prior to the outbreak of war in 1939, and (iii) the 8ft 0in wide vehicles, of which there are two classes, the SA and Q1.'

The SAs began to appear in November 1941. They were very different to anything seen on London streets up to now, for these 43 vehicles had been destined for Durban and Johannesburg and had been diverted by the government to London. Of these, 25 were Leylands, the rest AECs. The bodies were by Metro-Cammell and this common combination might have been thought to fit in well with London practice. In reality there were many differences, ranging from the 8ft width to the various features provided on vehicles intended to operate in far hotter climes than the Ilford area, which was where they found themselves.

A return to the STL class might be thought odd now that the RT had established itself but these were standard Regent 0661 chassis which had originally been intended for London but had not been delivered owing to wartime restrictions. The government

Left:
A Manchester Leyland Titan exchanges its home town destination blinds for London ones prior to taking up service from Hendon garage on the 13 in what is thought to be a posed publicity shot.

Right:
A standard former LGOC ST on loan to Trent. The rear of a Midland Red SOS built for Trent can just be seen. *A. D. Packer*

decided to allow manufacturers to finish them and other such vehicles, completion of which had been frozen, and they took charge of allocating them. Chiswick built bodies for their 34 'unfrozen' Regents, which looked very like the standard roof-box product, although internally they were very austere. In addition 14 of them had no roof route number box and nothing at all at the rear. The loss of the roof-box was no great tragedy, although it looked a bit odd, as by this time a restricted display had been brought in for all London buses; all the information had to be contained within the 'via' box and even this space was cut down. Trams and trolleybuses, less generous with their information anyhow, were unaffected.

Of these new STL bodies, 20 were of lowbridge layout — the first, indeed the only, more or less standard lowbridge bodies of its own design LT ever owned. They looked like proper STLs and were among the best proportioned of any lowbridge design, although, like their highbridge brothers, the single-skin roofs, absence of interior panelling and wooden-framed seats were well below the standards Londoners had come to expect. Some of the highbridge bodies, which followed on from 12 similar ones produced a little earlier to replace war-damaged bodies, were put on to the new chassis, the buses being numbered STL2648-81, registrations FXT 371-404; others were fitted to older chassis. Conversely, some of the new chassis gained older STL bodies of various types. Despite being painted red they were all sent to work in the Country Area, not being repainted green until 1944–7.

The 11 new members of the STD class, Nos 101–111, were even less like their predecessors than the new STLs. The Ministry of Supply had specified that bodies built during the war should be as austere as possible in order to conserve materials for the war effort, and STD101 carried the first such body to be produced. Built by Park Royal it bore no resemblance to the high quality standard LT prewar designs. Curves were kept to a minimum, as were opening windows, and there was just one route indicator, which was at the front. Interiors were stark and the rear window upstairs which, according to custom, served as the emergency exit, was unglazed. Side indicators were soon fitted because without them prospective passengers held up the bus by asking the conductor where it was going. The chassis was the Leyland Titan TD7. The unfrozen STDs spent their entire careers at Victoria (GM) garage where they were a familiar sight on the 137.

No new single-deckers appeared during the war years but 253 of various types were converted to 'Standee' layout which meant fitting the seats longitudinally, thus allowing up to 20 standing passengers.

1942

The last 'prewar' RT, No 151, entered service on 1 February 1942. Chelverton Road, Putney, lost many of its services during the war and so a number of the RTs were transferred to Victoria garage where they became most familiar on route 52. Later they worked from other garages but they were always chiefly associated with the two at Putney and when my father and I walked back from Barnes Bridge after watching the 1947 Boat Race, I was amazed at the almost

Left:
Newly delivered RT95 stands ahead of an STL at the Putney terminus of the 14. *G. Robbins collection*

Below:
An only slightly posed picture of the mobile staff canteen at Aldgate bus and trolleybus station, 5 September 1942. *Topical*

Right:
Bristol B1 at the Greenford terminus of route 97. *A. M. Wright*

continuous procession of RT2s which passed us along the Upper Richmond Road.

The lowbridge STL bodies, designed in 1941, did not enter service until 1942. None were fitted to unfrozen chassis, instead they went on to earlier ones whose bodies had been destroyed in the Blitz. All were painted red but they went into both Central and Country Area service, either augmenting routes already worked by lowbridge STs and STLs, or replacing single-deckers.

Although the Blitz was over and relatively few Nazi bombers now attacked London, the war effort still demanded great sacrifice. All Green Line services finished at the end of September. In order to reduce fuel consumption to a minimum, experiments were made with gas produced by burning anthracite in a trailer towed behind the bus. 20 STs from Grays garage in the Country Area were so equipped from June 1942, being the first major conversion.

Only a few months after the arrival of RT151 more new buses began to enter LT service. They were, however, inferior in every respect to the RT. B1-9 were Bristols, prewar K5Gs with Gardner engines, further examples of the unfrozen bus and the very

first Bristols seen in regular London service. They were fitted with Park Royal bodies, pretty well identical to those of the unfrozen STDs. The Bristols were sent to Hanwell garage where they remained throughout their careers and thus were never seen in central London.

The AECs, Leylands and Bristols were the prelude to a fleet of over 700 buses delivered under emergency wartime conditions, a fleet which we might charitably call a hiccup in the continuing development of the London bus, for it fell way below the standards Londoners had come to expect. Its life was short, much shorter than the average achieved by its prewar predecessors, many of whom outlasted it, although a fair proportion of it found employment elsewhere in one form or another after being disposed of by LT.

Both AEC and Leyland, far and away the most popular makes in both London and the provinces, were too occupied with war work to resume bus production, as was LT itself at its Chiswick works, at the new works at Aldenham, which had been built for the never completed Northern Line extension to Bushey, and elsewhere. The 23 was the only other central London Guy route. The G class eventually

Constructed from two old Central Line motor cars, with frames shortened and placed back to back, it was fitted with a Gardner diesel engine and whether working off the live rail or on diesel-electric power it could haul 600 tons on the level or 300 tons on gradients up to 1 in 34.

1943

As the war continued it became obvious that Guy could not supply all the double-deck bus requirements and so a second manufacturer, Daimler, was allowed to resume production. However no Daimler had arrived in London by the end of 1943 and the capital had to make do with more Guys. These had longer bonnets to accommodate the bigger 6LW engine if it was fitted — which it never was in London — a slightly modified Park Royal body and wooden slatted seats. In this they represented a nadir in standards of comfort, but in wartime passengers were prepared to grin and bear it. Like most of their class they were sent to work in the suburbs of east London. After the initial allocation of Guys to Tottenham garage, the next batch was sent to the western suburbs of Hanwell and Alperton. This, however, was to be an exception, for the Guys were very much associated

reached 435. They were fitted with a variety of bodies. The first were Park Royals, exactly the same as those on the STD and B classes, but others were given bodies built by Weymann, Northern Counties, Massey, a slightly altered Park Royal version and one Northern Coachbuilders, the latter being fitted to G30 after its original Park Royal body had been destroyed by enemy action. On the Underground a little-noticed pioneer appeared. This was DEL120, the prototype diesel-electric service locomotive. It is more accurately described as an electro-diesel.

with east London and the great majority was always based there. No G was ever allocated to a garage south of the river, indeed their only regular appearance on the south bank was on the short stretch of route 76 between Waterloo and Westminster bridges.

More Country Area garages and some Central Area ones began to operate gas producer buses in 1943. As gas was seen as an alternative fuel to petrol, rather than diesel, STs were chosen ——as in the Central Area — along with some single-deck Ts. Although Croydon operated some on the 197, like most people the ones I remember best were those which operated out of Camberwell garage on the 36, a route we travelled on between Victoria and Paddington when on our way to stay with my Aunt Agnes near

Shrewsbury. They lasted in this form for less than two years, being both underpowered and unreliable, and were converted back as soon as the fuel situation improved.

A further example of wartime stringency was the appearance of a number of new Guys and some overhauled standard buses, trams and trolleys in a livery of brown and cream. I recall that the brown wasn't so very different to that used on roofs, although more than one shade was used. Roofs had changed from silver when bauxite had been substituted for aluminium as a primer, both because it was cheaper and also made buses less visible from the air. That this was very necessary was tragically illustrated when an ST was machine-gunned in east London and its driver killed.

1944

If Londoners had believed that, with the end of the Blitz, the war turning round in favour of the Allies with the entry of the USA after Pearl Harbor, the defeat of the Germans in North Africa, the USSR standing firm at Leningrad and Stalingrad, and then D-Day, the worst was over, then the sudden onslaught of the pilotless flying bombs (the V1 'Doodlebugs') in June 1944 blew that illusion asunder. It was ironic that the trolleybus fleet, which had suffered so little in the Blitz, should suffer so much from these new weapons. Although V1s could be caught by RAF fighters, if they fired at them at too close a range then the resulting explosion could destroy the fighter too. By the time a doodlebug had reached Croydon it had evaded both anti-aircraft guns and Fighter Command and we would listen with dread for the distinctive note of its engine to cease suddenly. If it did, then we dived for the nearest cover.

Bexleyheath depot was virtually destroyed by a V1 on 29 June, along with 12 of its trolleybuses; the rest being either seriously or slightly damaged. Next month West Ham depot and works was hit twice, no less than 108 vehicles being damaged on the first occasion; even more, 154, on the second, although only one was destroyed.

As in the Blitz of 1940-1 so it was a local bus garage which suffered the most from a V1 attack. Elmers End was hit on 18 July: seven people died, 31 buses and a Green Line Q converted to an ambulance were destroyed, 19 other buses and nine converted coaches had their bodies wiped out. Three trams from Telford Avenue, a Feltham and two ex-Walthamstow cars, were damaged beyond repair at Kennington in August.

Even more terrifying were the V2s, the first guided missiles to be used in war. These were launched on London in September 1944. They flew at heights and speeds way beyond those of any ordinary aircraft and simply dropped out of the sky. There was no defence

against them, save that of capturing their launch sites, a task the Allied armies only accomplished some two months before the war ended.

New buses continued to be delivered in 1944. The long awaited Daimlers began to enter service in the late spring of 1944. D1-6 had lowbridge Duple bodies of typical austerity appearance and specification, and were sent to Merton garage to work route 127. Immediately after these the highbridge version of the D, again bodied by Duple, appeared. These too were sent to Merton and this large garage eventually housed all the wartime specification Daimlers.

Guys also continued to arrive in 1944. Although in very small numbers, they were a notable group for they went to Barking garage to work the 23, an east London route which operated from Becontree Heath right through the heart of the City of London and the West End to Oxford Street and Marylebone station. Slatted wooden seats remained the norm on new buses in 1944, although all would be upholstered later on.

The arrival of the austerity buses not only allowed the replacement of vehicles destroyed by enemy action, but occasionally others which were worn out or time-expired could be withdrawn. If an elderly LT or ST was badly damaged it was sometimes written off, whereas similar damage to a much newer STL or RT would be made good. In September 1944 the first withdrawal of an STL took place. This was, however, hardly a reflection on the general standard of the class for the vehicle in question, STL558, was a real oddity, being a former independent with a much-rebuilt outside-staircase body.

Whatever the trials and tribulations of war, most people try to carry on as normally as possible. It is difficult for those who have never lived in such times to understand the seemingly illogical lengths sometimes employed. Why waste effort and money on publicity photographs of new vehicles? Why worry about liveries? Surely it would have made sense to paint all PSVs in dull brown or grey? But it doesn't work like this, indeed making the best of the present

Above left:
The washing bay at Bexley depot on the morning of 27 June 1944 after the V1 hit. *LT*

Left:
The result of the bombing of Elmers End garage, 19 July 1944. *LT*

Above:
Despite the advent of Guys on route 23, LTs, including this splendid Bluebird example, continued to provide part of the allocation. *Alan Cross*

Below:
STLs and LTs, their windows fitted with anti-blast netting, lay over on the Embankment awaiting the evening rush hour. *Omnibus Soc*

and hoping and planning for a peaceful and progressive future becomes enormously important. The Beveridge Report promised a radically fairer Britain and, in its own way, LT responded to the general feeling that after the war better working and living conditions had to come about. Experiments were carried out in 1944 to ease the lot of the conductor by allowing him to sit down while collecting fares. Two trolleybuses, two STLs and RT97 (damaged by bomb blast) were rebuilt with power-operated sliding doors and circulating areas beside the seated conductor. All went into service initially in the Kingston area but proved unsuccessful. Loading took longer, something outside the conductor's control; it was also found that passengers could over-ride their stops and that the conductors could no longer keep an eye on what was going on upstairs.

Of course pay-as-you-enter did come in, decades later and under very different circumstances. Another

experiment of 1944 which would eventually become universal practice was the fitting of a District Line carriage with fluorescent lighting.

Strikes may seem an unlikely occurrence in wartime but there were a number at bus garages and trolleybus depots in the spring of 1944 in protest at working conditions and new, improved schedules. Both the schedules and the strikes were a sign that the end of the war was in sight. The army operated both buses and its own lorries until the dispute came to an end several days later.

1945

New buses of the G and D class continued to be delivered throughout 1945. At the very end of the year a further batch of Bristols joined the fleet. These 20 buses, B10–29, looked quite different to their predecessors in that they had a much lower and very

Below:
STL2482, repainted from red to green in 1944 and retaining full indicator blinds, working from Chelsham garage on the 403D at Tunbridge Wells.
Author's collection

elegant radiator, the standard postwar model which would become so familiar in Tilling fleets throughout the country. They had AEC engines, which were also fitted to most of the Daimlers, and identical Duple bodies — a good deal less spartan than earlier wartime ones, having curved domes, more opening windows and tubular steel seats with cushions covered in moquette instead of drab leathercloth or no cushions at all. B10-29 joined their brothers at Hanwell garage. All the earlier wartime buses had registrations beginning with G, but these later ones, Bristols, Daimlers and Guys, were all HGCs.

The war, of course, continued. Destruction from the air went on until the V2 missile sites were all captured. In March 15 Tilling STs, stored out of use beside Upton Park garage, were so badly damaged by a V2 falling nearby that they had to be written off. For all that, restrictions began to be lifted, beginning with those on headlamps in January 1945; no piloted enemy aircraft now attacked London and neither dark nor light made any difference to the V2s. Curiously the trams kept their masked headlamps, albeit in a modified form, until withdrawal in 1950-2. Just before VE-Day all lighting restrictions, inside and out, were abolished.

Traditionally, summer schedules were introduced early in May each year, one of the features being lots of extra buses on Sundays to places of entertainment and beauty spots. This meant lending red buses to help out in the Country Area and although the traffic levels of 1945 were not yet back to those of peacetime, they were better than anything since 1940.

The war in Europe ended officially on 8 May, but the celebrations began the day before and London and Londoners went mad. Buses, trams and trolleybuses carried vast numbers of revellers, though not at any great pace; schedules were thrown to the winds as the roads in the centre of London, and here and there in the suburbs, became jammed with joyful crowds.

Three months later Japan surrendered; the war was finally over. There were more celebrations and then LT got down to restoring peacetime conditions as quickly as possible. Inevitably this did not happen overnight.

Restrictions on a great variety of materials continued — for many years in some cases — and it took a while for all the soldiers, sailors and airmen to be demobbed. Three ex-servicemen opened an ironmonger's shop beside my local bus and tram stop and I used to peer through the door just to get a glimpse of these heroes. We regarded them as akin to knights returned from the Crusades.

Some 22,500 LT employees had joined the forces; 16,500 women had been recruited to replace them.

1946

Although passenger journeys had dropped by nearly 25 per cent at the height of the Blitz, by 1945 they were back to within 3 per cent of the prewar figure. The population of central London had declined by some 16 per cent, some 650,000 people — a trend which has continued to this day — but in the outer suburbs and beyond it had gone up by such an extent that Country Area routes were carrying a staggering increase of 90 per cent more passengers over the 1938-9 figure. To cope with this many single-deckers had been replaced by double-deckers.

426 LT staff were killed either at work or off duty; 2,873 were injured. 166 buses and coaches, 60 trams, 15 trolleybuses and 19 Underground carriages had been destroyed in air raids. Amongst the war work carried out by LT was the manufacture of over 700 Halifax four-engined bombers, the last one being named *London Pride* by Lord Ashfield.

Later, evening services began again on some routes before the summer of 1945 was out, while the winter schedules saw a further improvement. Although other operators resumed some coach services to the seaside, there had been no announcements about the restoration of the Green Line network; this, however, was not far away.

The first two postwar Green Line routes — 715 Hertford-Oxford Circus-Guildford and 720 Aldgate-Bishop's Stortford — began on 6 February 1946, both operated by demobbed 10T10s. The rest of the network, now numbered in the 700 series, was back in operation by late June and with it the familiar Ts, TFs and Qs. Livery was Lincoln green and white, the latter soon giving way to pale green. White and black destinations soon changed to black and yellow, which together with gold on green side boards gave the Green Line an added air of distinction. The network was soon doing as much and more business compared with prewar days, and the particularly heavily patronised routes out of Aldgate restarted with double-deck operation. The vehicles chosen were a curious bunch – 37 austerity Daimlers. Admittedly these D class buses were brand new but they were still built to later wartime specification and were not very comfortable. They were joined after a few months by a few prewar STLs.

A rather more suitable choice might have been yet another variation on the STL theme, if only there had been enough of them. Production of the STL was supposed to have ended in 1939 but in the event the war prolonged it for almost eight years, off and on. The very last went into service at the beginning of 1946. These 20 buses, coded 18STL20, although entering service before the last of the Gs and Ds, had chassis much in common with the unfrozen STLs. Their Weymann bodies showed little sign of wartime skimping — the only note of austerity was the one-piece indicators fitted back and front. Had they been given standard three-piece ones, they would have looked a lot more like a traditional London bus. The late prewar and immediate postwar combination of the AEC Regent and the Weymann body has become a classic: one thinks of the long-lived Brighton examples of 1939, one of which has been preserved. These STLs were fine looking vehicles — but only the livery had much to do with LT traditions. They spent all their short lives in LT ownership working in the Country Area; three were delivered in red livery, but this was changed to green before 1946 was out. Numbered STL2682–2701, HGC 215–234, they were sent to Watford High Street garage. Like many another enthusiast I journeyed all the way to Watford in order to record them in my *abc*.

The arrival of new AECs by no means brought to an end the delivery of Daimlers. Shortly after the last austerity Daimler went into service, D182 was delivered — the first of 100 with similar chassis but with Park Royal bodies and built to more or less peacetime specifications. This body was very similar to that fitted to a batch of Southdown Leyland PD1s. Even though they had full three-piece indicators the Park Royal Daimlers seemed to us bus spotters to be

firmly in the austerity camp, not least because of their painted radiators. They were sent to Sutton garage and that meant the Morden area in particular, within cycling distance of home, was awash with Ds from Merton and Sutton garages. My friend Hicks, who lived at Carshalton, copped all 281. D182–281 sported a new livery, basically all red with cream bands above the upper and lower deck windows. It was part of the move away from the magnificent red, white, silver and black of prewar days to the sombre, virtually all red of 1950.

If LT was not yet able to order buses to its own, precise, specific requirements, then at least it could choose from manufacturers' standard provincial peacetime catalogues. So after the Weymann-bodied Regents came 65 all-Leyland PD1 Titans. Another classic design, they were put into the STD class, 112–176, HGF 990–999 and HLW 51–105, following on from the prewar TD4s and the unfrozen TD7s. They had a full set of route indicators at the front — although the actual display was still restricted — including roof number box, which made them instantly look like a London bus. They were painted in yet another livery variation, but one which was

Below:
LT1142 and new TD9, Golders Green. *D. A. Jones*

Left:
T733 of the first batch of postwar Ts working from Uxbridge garage. *IAL*

Below:
A well-laden Tilling ST swings round Parliament Square ahead of a spanking new Talbot.

Left:
All-Leyland PD1 STD119 about to set off for Loughton from Victoria.

Above right:
Green Line D161 at Aldgate bus station. *G. F. Ashwell*

Right:
T579 of Reigate enters Regent Street on the 711 in pursuit of two LTs.

standard for the next four years: mostly red, black wings, a cream centre band and cream upper deck window frames except at the back. Some actually worked past the end of our road, from Croydon garage on route 115, alongside Sutton's Park Royal-bodied Ds, but they were soon transferred away and I've never seen a picture of one so employed. In most memories they are associated with Victoria (GM) — on the 77 and 137 — and Loughton (L) and the 38a. The postwar STDs were delivered between August and December 1946.

Yet more new buses delivered in 1946 were the first single-deckers since the CRs of 1939. If it seemed the STL class was destined to go on acquiring new members *ad infinitum*, what of the T? The first member of the class dated back to November 1929; nearly 17 years later production was resumed with a batch of 50 Central Area buses, T719-768 (HGF 809–858), coded 14T12. They had nice looking, if slightly old-fashioned, Weymann 35-seat front-entrance bodies. Slide vent windows gave them a somewhat provincial appearance but there were already so many variations all lumped into the T class that they looked perfectly at home. Because of shortages they did not actually replace any older vehicles, although a number of Ts had already disappeared from the fleet, largely as a consequence of the war.

The final buses of the interim period between austerity types and the postwar standards, began to arrive in December 1946. These were 31 Leyland (Leylands formed a far higher proportion of the single-deck fleet than the double) PS1 Tigers and were put into a new class (although the classification had been used before), being numbered TD1-31 (HGF 959-989). Their bodies were identical to those fitted to the contemporary 14T12s.

Below ground the wartime brake on expansion was released in December 1946 when the Central Line tunnels, used for war work, were opened and trains began to run as far as Stratford, emerging out into the open just before the station where it was possible to cross the platform to join LNER stopping services.

We cannot end our look at 1946 without reference to the Victory Parades with which London celebrated the return of peace. These took place on 8 June and consisted of a procession of marching men and women and also a mechanised one. My father, despite having been a driver in Allenby's army in World War 1, preferred to watch the march past but we did catch part of the mechanised one, amongst which were four buses, two from the provinces which had helped out in London in 1940, and two RTs, Nos 4 and 39.

Below:
Park Royal-bodied RT214, one of many roof-box RTs allocated to Croydon Garage, sets off from Thornton Heath Pond.

1947

Above:
Former Great Eastern Railway 'F5' class 2-4-2T No 67213 with the 11.32 Epping-Ongar alongside a Central Line tube train. *Brian Morrison*

1947 was a year to gladden the heart of LT management, staff and customers. On Saturday 10 May the long awaited first postwar RT entered service. Numbered 402, even though the highest 'prewar' RT number was 151, it established a precedent for the class that meant, for instance, that RT4230 could appear over three years before RT3836. Chiswick was so inundated with overhaul work after the long years of wartime neglect that it would never again take on a production run, and so Park Royal and Weymann had been contracted to build the first postwar bodies for the RT. Park Royals were to run from 152 to 401 and Weymanns from 402 onwards. It so happened that the first Weymann bus was ready before the first Park Royal one — RT152 entered service on 23 May — and thus RT402 became the prototype of what was arguably the largest standardised class of bus to operate in any city, worldwide, although this honour really belongs to prewar RT1. RTs 152 and 402 went to Leyton for route 10, replacing open staircase LTs.

The chassis of the postwar RT was similar to its predecessor, but the engine was a new one, rather more powerful and with a quite different sound, much less of a throbbing roar. Visually the differences between the pioneer members of the class and the postwar ones, the 3RT3s, were not great, chiefly the

level instead of drooping cab window, the front destination indicator below instead of above the 'via', and no roof-box number indicator at the back. It was metal-framed, instead of composite, and its parts were designed to be totally interchangeable. Internally it was superb, absolutely up to date and quite the most luxurious and well-appointed bus on the road. The smell of a brand new or newly overhauled RT was something which one never forgets. Visually John Gillham, the oracle of class 5 in all matters pertaining to LT at Winterbourne Primary School, described it as 'looking like a trolleybus'. And certainly both types shared similar smooth lines and livery.

By the end of 1947 171 new RTs had entered service and I had seen and even travelled on quite a few of them, for many were sent to Croydon and Bromley garages to replace time-expired former Tilling and LGOC STLs and STs. Perhaps surprisingly they weren't all put on the trunk routes to the West End and the City but could be found monopolising such purely local ones as the 197, 130 and 119. They were to stay on the former for more than a quarter of a century. They also saw off the Croydon STDs, the only class of

Leyland buses ever to work from Croydon until the T class Titans of a later generation. The STDs went northeastwards to Loughton and Leyton.

However 171 new buses was nowhere near sufficient to take over from the swathes of LTs, STs and STLs ruthlessly removed from service, sometimes for overhaul but much more often for scrap. In desperation, but with rather more justification, the scenes of 1940 were repeated when, beginning in October, vehicles were hired from many sources to make good the shortages. This time they were coaches, a total of 350, and ranged from the antique to the brand new and appeared on routes normally worked by red double-deckers.

Left:
Aldenham works with four STLs, an ST
and a Bluebird LT. *Photo Centre*

Below left:
Central Area Q167, RT274, T16 and
an LTC parked outside Wembley
Stadium. *IAL*

Right:
The classic RT upper deck, still familiar
56 years after it first appeared.

Below:
A Grey-Green prewar Leyland Tiger
coach, one of 350 vehicles hired by
London Transport to help out with
vehicle shortages, stands alongside an
ST at London Bridge, 27 October
1947. In the 1980s and 1990s Grey-
Green would become an operator of
bus services in London. *Topical*

A startling sight in Katharine Street, Croydon was
an ST in blue and yellow. Not even Gillham could
explain this apparition. Years later I discovered that
this was one of the Inter-Station buses which had been
used to replace or augment the one-and-a-half-deck
Cubs built for this service. Now the STs could return
to ordinary service. Officially they were all modified
internally and repainted back into red livery before
this happened but the one I saw must have worked
briefly in its Inter-Station condition before Chiswick
got its hands on it. More STs re-appeared to help out
with the chronic shortage of vehicles, a number of the
Tilling variety being put back into passenger service.

The final vehicles of the first batch of TDs took up
work in June but no single-deckers were withdrawn;
they were all needed. Even the private hire LTCs
turned up on Green Line relief duties.

Many of the wartime buses still had wooden seats
and some, but by no means all, had these replaced by
cushioned ones in 1947. Other reminders and relics of
wartime days remained — restricted route indicators
on all buses, bomb sites which in the summer
sprouted luxuriant weeds and wild flowers, while
petrol rationing meant there were few private cars to
inhibit the progress of buses, trams and trolleybuses.

A sign of better times ahead was the opening on 14

December of the Central Line extension from Leytonstone to Woodford and Newbury Park in place of LNER (in two weeks' time they would have become British Railways) steam trains.

As the year ended so did the 14-year existence of the London Transport Passenger Board. The Transport Act which brought about the Nationalisation of the railways also brought into existence the London Transport Executive, although to the vast majority of its passengers the only difference, if they bothered to look, was a change in the legal lettering on the buses, trams and trollies.

1948

The London Passenger Transport Board ceased to exist at the end of 1947, becoming, with Nationalisation, the London Transport Executive (LTE). Lord Ashfield was the driving force; with Frank Pick he had raised LT to its pre-eminent position. He had retired as Chairman in October 1947 and died just over a year later.

Production of new buses steadily increased in 1948 as did withdrawal of standard vehicles from the prewar LT, ST and STL classes. Perhaps the most significant new bus was RTL501. Leyland had been

contracted at the beginning of 1947 to build its own version of the RT. Like the prewar STD this would closely resemble its AEC counterpart. The Leyland version came in two widths, standard and outsize. Despite the Ministry of Transport having recently sanctioned an increase in width from 7ft 6in to 8ft (the SA class of trolleybuses intended for South Africa were the very first eight-footers to operate in London, but only in the suburbs) it was not considered certain that some of central London's narrowest streets would permit two eight-footers to pass each other without dire results for pedestrians and other traffic. Thus Leyland was asked to build 500 8ft wide buses complete with bodies and 1,000 7ft 6in wide chassis. The first of the latter went into service in June 1948. The resemblance to the RT was so close that it actually carried a Park Royal body intended for RT657. The chassis was a much modified Titan PD2/1 fitted with a radiator, which was instantly recognisable as Leyland, but of similar dimensions to the AEC one on RTs. The Leyland 7ft

Below:
Bristol/ECW lowbridge K5G at Victoria on the 38 alongside an STL on the 16. *IAL*

Above:
Conversation piece at Kingston bus station alongside Mann Egerton TDs 127/118.

Right:
Mann Egerton-bodied T791 representing the final 15T13 version of this class, 10T10 T574 and postwar STL2689. *IAL*

6in chassis was modified to accept the standard RT body, and some other components were identical to those on RT chassis. RTL501 was so numbered because it had originally been intended that the 8ft wide Titans would be RTLs 1-500; in the event they were put into a separate class.

The production Leylands went into service from December 1948, but these were noticeably different in appearance to the prototype, as they had Leyland 8ft wide bodies. We'll return to them but meanwhile we must record the first Country Area RTs. These arrived in July, Nos 597-603, and were sent to Tring. More followed, to a variety of garages north and south of

the river. RTs 152-401 had HLW registration letters, 402 onwards HLX. These ended at RT621, 622 being JXC 430 (RTL501 was JXC 20).

Because so many new buses were needed to replace the virtually defunct LTs, STs and many of the STLs, suffering acutely from the neglect of the war years, Park Royal and Weymann were unable to supply all LT's needs so other builders were contracted to build bodies for RTs: Craven in Yorkshire and Saunders on the Isle of Anglesey.

The first of 120 Craven RTs, No 1402, arrived in September 1948. It looked very different to any other RT, being basically a standard Craven product

Left:
Craven-bodied RT1406 at Croxley
Green. *F. G. Reynolds*

Below left:
Red RT767 at Horsham Carfax
loaned to Crawley Garage to work a
former Hants & Sussex route.

Right:
Weymann-bodied 3RT3 RT972 of
Leatherhead garage passing Reeves
Corner, Croydon, and a Wolseley of
the type used by the Metropolitan
Police in the immediate postwar
years, on the long run from
Chelsham to Guildford.

modified slightly, fitted with RT seats and roof-box indicator, and adapted to fit the RT chassis. Its shape was different, it had a five-bay window layout, a more curvaceous back and a flatter front. We contemporary bus spotters found the Cravens an interesting variation but I don't think anyone thought them a patch visually on the standard RT. Craven RTs were distributed all over the network, painted both red and green; we had a few of the former delivered new locally to Elmers End and Croydon.

What the 1948 *abc* was pleased to call 'the single-deck version of the RT' entered service in the early part of 1948. These were the very last members of the T class, Nos 769-798, HLX 439-468. Painted in the now outdated green and white, despite the fact that ancient rebuilt Ts and single deck LTs and contemporary RTs had substituted cream for white, these 30 buses, coded 15T13, had 31-seat bodies built by Mann Egerton. They were handsome looking vehicles, but were hardly the single-deck equivalent of the RT, despite their modified Regal III chassis with air-operated pre-selective gearboxes, fluid transmission, 9.6 litre engines, and interior finished in RT style. All were sent north of the river to the garages of Two Waters and Leavesden Road, Watford. At the beginning they were associated with Hertfordshire and later Essex, although many later migrated south of the river, particularly to Sussex at Crawley.

The 1/1TD2s was the second group of 100 Leyland PS1 Tigers which began to arrive in the autumn of 1948. Close relations to the 15T13s, they had Mann Egerton bodies identical to the Ts except that, being in the Central Area, the Metropolitan Police (a body who in PSV matters never seemed to have quite got over the trauma of the replacement of the horse)

refused to allow the fitting of a sliding door. They were painted in the new standard all-red, with a smidgen of cream, and, numbered TD32-131 (JXC 225-324), were sent to a number of garages, allowing the withdrawal of many single-deck LTs and some of the earlier Ts.

The arrival of Ian Allan's *abc of London Transport* in 1948 was a tremendous boon to enthusiasts. Written by S. L. Poole, here for the first time was set out just about all one wished to know about the contemporary London bus scene, with a bit of history thrown in. I still have my original — somewhat less than mint condition copy — second edition, which was a reprint of the first, both appearing in 1948. As with many contemporary railway 'ABCs' its cover featured a woodcut by A. N. Wolstenholme, not quite 100 per cent accurate for RT567 on route 46 seen alongside T637 on route 703 has the drooping window of the 'prewar' RT, but attractive for all that.

One more group of very welcome arrivals on the London scene must be recorded. In January the first of a new class of trolleybus arrived. This was the Q1, 77 of which had been on order since 1946. Described in the 1948 *abc* as 'the ultimate development of the standard trolleybus', they were very much in the LT tradition but improved in various respects, being 8ft wide, of five window-bay construction and more powerful with their MCW bodies mounted on BUT chassis. BUT was a joint selling organisation set up by AEC and Leyland; nevertheless the Q1s were basically of AEC design but assembled at Leyland's Ham factory, near Kingston. All were sent to Fulwell depot where they replaced the original London United Diddlers.

Despite the frustrations of continuing restrictions on new equipment and the need to keep outdated

Above:
Tilling STL83 about to be overtaken by recently delivered
RTL2 at Eltham. *Alan Cross*

1949

vehicles and rolling stock serviceable, in one sense
1948 was LT's finest year for it carried more
passengers — 4,675 million — than it ever had before
or would again. It was a year for optimists. We might
have been annihilated by the Australians on Don
Bradman's final tour, despite the valiant efforts of
Hutton, Washbrook, Edrich, Compton, Evans and
Alec Bedser, but we did stage the first postwar
Olympics, LT playing its part to the full by providing
transport for the competitors in anything from a little
CR to an ancient LT double-decker. Unemployment
was just a bad memory left over from the 1930s. We
had enough money to go out regularly and on holiday,
but probably not enough to afford personal transport,
nor the petrol coupons even if we did own a car, so
we went by bus, motor coach or train. So popular
were excursions out of London that red double-
deckers on loan to the Country Area became a
common sight on Sundays when every available green
bus was already out and about — a situation
inconceivable today.

If 1948 was a year when production of postwar
standard vehicles really began to take off, in 1949 it
became a flood ——no less than 1,592 being delivered,
a figure almost sufficient to have completely renewed
the fleet of Midland Red, that provincial giant which
covered a greater area of England than any other
company. It gives one some idea of the pre-eminence
of LT.

Three more new types appeared, although only one
was destined to last long. First came RTC1, a highly
glamorous innovation which fired the imaginations of
us schoolboys, although I saw it only once, in late
May when it worked briefly on the 708 which passed
through Croydon. RTC1 was the much-rebuilt RT97
and intended as a prototype for a fleet of double-
deck Green Line coaches. Not for the first time such a
concept failed, although it would eventually succeed.
RTC1 served only nine months in its intended role,
being then relegated to country bus duties and sold in
1955.

Another failure, equally interesting but visually of
much lower profile, was the SRT. It seemed to LT
that production of new bodies was going to outstrip
that of chassis and so it was decided that 300 STL

Right:
Metro-Cammell-bodied RTL968
crossing Putney Bridge.

Below:
Moorgate station; two Metropolitan
line trains about to depart, the
nearer, bound for Watford, is made
up of brown-liveried, compartment T
stock dating from the late 1920s,
whilst alongside is a P stock train for
Uxbridge. *R. E. Vincent*

chassis would be rebuilt to take RT-type bodies. The final, FJJ/FXT-registered batch dating from 1939 was chosen, their bodies being transferred to the STL2014-2188 group which had been given all-metal bodies; these were now in an advanced state of decay. The first SRTs entered service in April 1949. They met with a frosty reception from the crews who found the STL engines, perfectly adequate for the lighter original vehicle, lacking in power for the more than half a ton heavier SRT, while the brakes also gave trouble. Put to work on such trunk routes as the 35 from Camberwell garage, the 16 from Victoria and the 24 from Chalk Farm, as well as less demanding suburban ones, their lives were short and they were withdrawn in 1953-4, although, of course, their bodies lasted for decades longer, being transferred to new RT chassis. Production was cut short to end at 160.

The third new type was the long awaited 8ft wide Leyland. Classified RTW: the first, registered KGK 501, took up work from Tottenham garage in June 1949. The RTW was the truest descendant of the prewar STD for it too carried a Leyland body skilfully disguised to look like its AEC counterpart but giving its origins away in certain details. It has to be said it was a pretty convincing copy of what an 8ft wide RT would have been like if there had ever been one and you had to look hard to detect the tell-tale differences. Chief was the rear-end upper deck where some of the earlier RTWs had the standard and distinctive

Leyland guttering above the emergency window, curving upwards on the nearside, downwards on the off. Rubber stops either side of the indicator to cushion the emergency window should it be opened meant that the rear adverts had to be moved outwards and this, as well as the extra 6in width, instantly distinguished an RTW from an RT or an RTL. These are not matters of any great significance perhaps, but the spice of life to ardent bus spotters.

Among the many withdrawals were the last Tilling STs, although several were converted to mobile canteens, and one miraculously returned to passenger service in central London many years later, as we shall see. The last open staircase buses in normal service, the first group of LTs, were withdrawn in April although they and some Tillings lasted a little longer in the special events fleet.

One July afternoon, heading for Paddington aboard an STL on the 36, I was not a little surprised to see approaching as we turned out of the Edgware Road into Praed Street a shiny green RT on route 7 heading towards London Bridge. LT seemingly deemed the Central Area's need the greater and thus allocated a batch of new green RTs to Middle Row and also Mortlake garages, although only for a few weeks until sufficient new red buses became available.

Yet another supplier of RT-type bodies appeared on the scene in August when the first of 450 built by Metro-Cammell and fitted to RTLs 551-1000 started

Above left:
RTW116 of West Green Garage and D2 class trolleybus No 489 in Forest Road, Woodford. *R. E. Vincent*

Above:
SRT15 on the 24 approaching Parliament Square whilst a former West Ham car on the 36 rounds the curve from the Embankment to Westminster Bridge, pursued by a Feltham on the 18. *IAL*

Right:
SRT43 from Cricklewood Garage and RTL793 from Old Kent Road at Victoria. *Author's collection*

work. Although visually the only external difference from the Park Royal and Weymann version was a thicker moulding above the central cream band, variations in construction meant that these bodies always stayed on this batch of buses. Despite all these new buses, London was still desperately short of serviceable vehicles, and was able to secure the loan of new ECW-bodied Bristol double-deckers intended

for various Tilling bus companies. The Tilling group, like LT, was now part of the British Transport Commission. The first of some 190 had arrived before the end of 1948. LT also managed to secure further hired coaches from independent operators.

On the Underground the first of the 143 new R47 stock cars entered service on the District Line. All were motor cars. There were 91 new Tube cars, the

Above:
RTC1 at Grosvenor Bridge atop Victoria station.

Right:
An ST heads a long line of STs, LTs and a Tilling STL at Epsom Downs, performing some of their last duties.

1949 stock, built to the last prewar design; 21 of them were trailers, the rest UNDMs — which being translated means uncoupling non-driving motor car. This meant that you could actually drive them for short distances to enable uncoupling and shunting, not from a proper cab but from a control cabinet by the door and the guard's controls, thus saving space. These all went to work with the 1938 stock on the Northern and Bakerloo lines.

1950

Enter a new decade and, in several senses, a new era. Two of the three modern standard classes of double-deck bus inherited by LT from the General disappeared in January 1950. These were the ST and the LT. I think just about all enthusiasts had a special affection for the LTs in particular. The big six-wheelers, whether the pioneer open staircase version, the later ones with camel type front indicators, or the stylish Bluebirds, simply exuded personality. They had disappeared from Croydon in the autumn of 1948. On starting my new school, Whitgift Middle, in

September that year, one of the Elmers End
contingent would convey me each Wednesday and
Saturday afternoon from the centre of Croydon to the
playing fields at Sandilands, Addiscombe, where I
was initiated, with no great enthusiasm, into the
mysteries of scrums, line outs and fatal injuries — or
so I expected — but within a couple of weeks they
were all gone, replaced by RTs even newer than my
sparkling, mitre-embossed black blazer.

Petrol rationing also disappeared in 1950 and from
now on private motoring would steadily take away
many of its passengers from all forms of public
transport.

1950 was especially significant in LT's history for
it marked the final beginning of the end of its huge
tram fleet. The outbreak of war had prolonged the
life of the south London routes, but with the
production of the RT family now in full flood, there
were sufficient new buses to resume the tram
replacement programme. For various reasons it had
been decided that the trolleybus also had a limited
lifespan and in the autumn of 1950 Wandsworth
depot lost both its trams and trolleybuses, 75 RTs
taking over, while Clapham had some of its trams
replaced by 54 RTLs.

Not all the trams were scrapped, for Wandsworth
had been home to the relatively modern E3 class and
these went off to New Cross and Telford Avenue.
However for the older E1s the end had arrived and
these were driven to Penhall Road, Charlton, where a
large yard had been made ready to receive them.
Many buses also met their end there. Saturday 30

September was the day chosen for the tramway
replacement programme to begin and on the following
Monday, 2 October, E1 No 1656 was toppled over
and set alight. It was all over in about an hour.

A route operated by Wandsworth depot was the 31,
one of the three surviving North London ones, which
ran through Kingsway Subway. It had originally
terminated at Hackney but the prewar trolleybus
programme had seen it diverted to Islington. Now its
replacement bus service, the 170, resumed working to
Hackney but not through the Subway where there was
insufficient clearance. Buses did appear on the
Embankment for the first time, southbound they ran
over the tram lines, which were still used by many
services, and there was at least one accident where a
tram and bus collided. In all, six tram routes
disappeared, the 12, 26, 28, 31, 34 and the all night 3,
along with the 612 trolleybus. The 44 bus route
replaced both 12 and 612, restoring a state which had
existed before the trolleybuses had arrived, the others
being the 45, 168, 169, 170 and 288.

Wandsworth's RTs and Clapham's RTLs all entered
service displaying full indicator blinds. The first full
blinds had appeared in country buses in May and were
the first such since the early war years. There was also
a livery change around this time but far less welcome.

Cream upper-deck window frames disappeared leaving just a thin cream band between the upper and lower decks to relieve the vast expanse of red. The shock of seeing the first vehicle so painted, Catford's RT1679, which worked into Croydon on the 54, was considerable and although a brand new RT always looked splendid, from now on we had to rely on the acreage of adverts, front, sides and back, to brighten up the otherwise almost unrelieved red or green livery of the vast London fleet. Croydon also saw the first Country Area buses to have full indicator blinds when all Godstone's RTs, which worked the 409 and the 411, were so equipped. We also got our first RTWs, a batch being sent in June to Bromley garage to work the 119.

However, much more excitement awaited the RTW class when a series of tests took place that summer in central London. Temporarily allocated to garages which worked into the West End and the City, they appeared for the first time on a number of the routes with which they would later be associated. No fearful consequences for either traffic or pedestrians resulted from the extra 12in which two passing RTWs occupied and the ban on them appearing in Oxford Street, Shaftesbury Avenue, Threadneedle Street, etc was lifted. However they could not run alongside trams.

The curious situation where wartime Daimlers operated Green Line services was brought to an end in August 1950 when they were replaced by 36 RTs. These Romford buses, despite being identical inside to the standard vehicle, always looked particularly distinguished for they carried no external adverts, had a pale green central band and a raised Green Line motif between the decks. The displaced Ds went to join their brothers at Merton and I saw several of them still operating from there in green livery before they were repainted.

The last petrol-engined STL had gone in 1949 and vast inroads into the oil-engined fleet were made in 1950. At the beginning of the year there were 2,110 licensed for service but by the end this had shrunk to 903, the biggest drop ever and a drastic decline from the maximum of 2,620 at the end of 1946. Remarkably a brand new STL body was under construction at Chiswick Works. The foreman of the experimental shop, Arthur Sainsbury, jointly with LT had patented a system using prefabricated units and this was used to provide a new body, albeit in pre-1946 red and white livery, for STL2477, ELP 154. Nicknamed the 'Meccano Set' it bore some resemblance to a standard STL and ran for four years in London before being sold. It, and its method of construction, remained unique.

Two further classes were on the way out by the end of 1950. LT's last petrol-engined buses, the little Inter-Station yellow and blue Leyland Cubs,

Above:
An extremely down at heel former General STL39 ending its days on learner duty. *IAL*

Right:
RLH17 climbing past the Pilgrims Way north of Westerham.

C106-113, were withdrawn, although they came back in the following March to operate a BEA service between Waterloo and Heathrow, while the first wartime buses, members of the G class, were also delicensed. Although only a stop-gap measure, one somehow hadn't expected any of the austerity classes to go just yet. Both types were replaced by members of the RT family, although STLs were also used to displace Gs. Amongst the first routes to lose its Guys was the 76 — one of only two West End routes operated by Tottenham garage. Yet a new Guy entered the fleet in 1950. This was G436, KGK 981, an Arab with a standard Park Royal-designed provincial body and a big Meadows 10.35 litre engine. Like the 'Meccano set' STL, it seems to have been a unique experiment which had no influence on future vehicle policy.

By the end of 1950 the RT fleet number had reached as high as 4264 (to Croydon, of course!), although there were many gaps yet to be filled and the quite extraordinary, and to this day unique, total of 1,828 new buses (if one counts the final 18 SRTs) had been delivered.

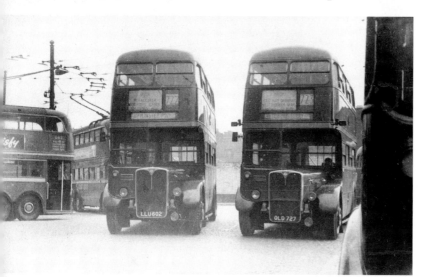

Left:
Green Line RT3243 and 4507 and trolleybuses at Aldgate.

Below:
RTW406 takes up work on London's most famous route.

Above:
An immaculate Feltham, No 2156, heads through Streatham with an early STL following respectfully behind. *Alan Cross*

Right:
A wooden-bodied rake of District Hurst Nelson pre-1914 stock passing a semaphore signal on the East London Line. *IAL*

1951

The beginning of 1951 saw two endings. The very last roof number box bus, Saunders RT4267, was delivered to Streatham garage in February. On the night of 6-7 January the second stage of the tram replacement programme took place when all of Clapham's remaining trams and many of Telford Avenue's were replaced by RTLs and RTs respectively. A third tram depot, Brixton, also began operating buses — RTs. Mention of Telford Avenue immediately brings the Felthams to mind. Despite being in their 20th year these magnificent vehicles were still in excellent condition and it seemed inconceivable that they could meet a fiery end in downtown Charlton. Leeds agreed and bought the lot. They were already being withdrawn from service in London, older cars filling in for them for the last few months of the routes on which they were normally

employed: the 8, 10, 16, 18 and 20. Of these the 8, 10 and 20 disappeared on 6-7 January, along with the 2, 4, 6, 22 and 24. Trams had now disappeared from Wimbledon and the last bit of LUT track, while the Tooting route had been the very first to be electrified by the LCC in 1903. Some E3s were sent to Norwood depot to work the 16 and 18 and to allow room at Telford Avenue for conversion to a bus garage; some E1s were broken up, while others took over from the Felthams on Telford Avenue's remaining routes. I was very indignant at the loss of my beloved Felthams, especially as their substitutes were run down ex-LCC E1s, the oldest cars in London.

Replacement bus routes were the 50, 57, 57A, 95, 104, 155B/W, 189, 189A and 287. The curious suffixes to the 155 indicated whether they preceded around the Embankment inwards by way of Blackfriars or Westminster (replacing the 2 and 4 trams), but they caused only confusion and were soon dropped.

In February RTWs first began to operate regularly through central London, Clayhall and Willesden garages putting them on the 8 and 8A. More Guys and STLs were withdrawn as new RTs and RTLs arrived and an interesting development saw the 'Tunnel' STLs begin to give way to ordinary buses, consequent upon the lowering of the roadway through the Blackwall Tunnel.

I was suffering from a bad cold on the weekend of 7-8 April and thus wasn't able to witness the end of the trams which had been so much part of my life. My parents went and reported on the large crowds, a feature of every tram abandonment. Not only did the 16 and 18 routes — which at peak periods needed no less than 80 cars — disappear, but also our local 42 which ran between Thornton Heath High Street and Coombe Road, Croydon. Thornton Heath depot, from which I could hear the trams setting off each morning, had been closed for several months, demolished and a new bus garage erected on the site. The old Purley depot, where one could catch glimpses of non-windscreen-fitted E1s (I had at first thought them war casualties) in store for many years after such trams had last carried passengers, was cleared out and Thornton Heath's allocation moved in. Now that had gone too, although the building was to remain, the new home for Bedford lorries belonging to Schweppes. The very last tram was No 839, a rehabilitated E1, chartered by the Croydon and Purley Chambers of Commerce, suitably decorated, which ran from Purley to Thornton Heath, completing its journey sometime after midnight.

The new Thornton Heath bus garage had its entrance round the back in Whitehall Road, the road next to ours, where my friend John lived; his father was a policeman who had been on the roof of the sweet factory in Croydon on the night of the notorious Derek Bentley and Christopher Craig fatal shooting. The trams had made their entry straight out into the main London Road, the new arrangement avoided possible traffic congestion.

So on Monday 9 April I waited for a 109 or 190 bus to take me to school and when one appeared I was doubly disappointed for not only was it secondhand, being a hand-me-down RT from Wandsworth which had converted to RTLs, it was also full up. I can't recall any occasion when I hadn't managed to squeeze on to a tram; now it was quite common to have two buses pass by full up. Also it cost me more money; on a Feltham if one was quick and lacked scruples, one could nip down the front staircase when one heard the footsteps of the conductor ascending the rear one and alight without paying.

The next abandonment took place on 10 July, a Tuesday, when two termini, Waterloo and Tooley Street near London Bridge, each lost their sole routes, the 68 and 70 respectively, both of which served Greenwich. Although the trams lived at New Cross the replacement bus routes, the 70 (one of only two bus routes which took the same number as the tram route it replaced), 70A and the 188, operated temporarily out of a new garage at Peckham. Tram route 72, briefly extended during stage 1 to Borough, now went back to its Savoy Street terminus.

Stage 5 arrived on the night of 6-7 October when 99 trams from Camberwell depot were replaced by 109 buses. Routes 36, 56, 58, 60, 62, 66, 84 and the all night 7 disappeared. Most of these were operated by the HR(hilly route)2 class trams designed to cope with the steep gradients, the climb through the sylvan surroundings up to exclusive Dulwich culminating in

the four-track Dog Kennel and a swoop down past the exotica contained within the Horniman Museum. The HR2s were amongst the most modern London trams and too good to burn, even at this late stage, and were sent for service elsewhere, including the 35 Kingsway Subway route. It was about this time I had my one and only ride through the Subway, a unique tram experience, to dive from the bright sun of the Embankment into the gloom beneath Waterloo Bridge, curving round before the long straight stretch beneath Kingsway itself and to alight at the intermediate Aldwych, just as though it was an underground railway station. In its new guise Camberwell depot became known as Walworth bus garage, because there was already an existing Camberwell bus garage.

On the opposite side of the river the South bank of the Thames was occupied that summer by the Festival of Britain. A marvellous extravaganza, marking the centenary of the Great Exhibition held in the Crystal Palace, but also a final turning back on the years of austerity. Shiny RTs seemed part of the brave new world the Festival promised, trams did not. Elderly STLs didn't either really, but nevertheless no fewer than 183 of the class had been overhauled and were put to work on eight of the nine special services in connection with the Festival.

Although not as old as the STLs, nor for that matter the prewar TD4 STDs, the 11 unfrozen TD7 STDs, very unpopular with crews, were all taken out of service by March, 1951 and subsequently sold.

1951 was the year when the true single-deck version of the RT, the RF, entered service. Destined to be almost as long lived, this was based on the AEC Regal IV underfloor-engined chassis and had a body designed, of course, by LT, and built by Metro-Cammell. The first 25 were only 27ft 6in long (the remainder were 30ft), and like all the class, 7ft 6in wide. RF1-25, LUC201-225, were 35-seat private hire

coaches, fitted with glass cant panels and painted in an attractive Lincoln green and grey livery with red lettering and lining out. Immediately after them the production Green Line coaches began entering service. These were destined to replace all prewar coaches and initially numbered 263 vehicles, although there were subsequent transfers to and from the Central and Country Area fleets. They seated 39 passengers.

Concurrently with the first RFs an 8ft-wide version entered service. This was the RFW. It was quite unlike any other London single-decker, having an ECW body of unique design with 39 proper coach seats — Green Line coaches were really only glorified buses. There were 15 of them and they joined the private hire fleet.

At the other extreme a couple of Country Area lowbridge STs were transferred to the Central Area to work the 230.

On the Underground the first five car trains of modern P stock had begun operating on the Circle Line in 1947, replacing older stock, including that with hand worked doors. One of the reasons I found travelling on the Underground scary as a small child was rattling through tunnels with the sliding doors partly open; I had nightmares about falling out. By the beginning of 1951 the last rake of these ancient, wooden-bodied cars dating back to the 1920s and beyond had finally been withdrawn.

1952

1952 opened with the largest number of trams taken out of service in one fell swoop so far; before the summer was out they would all be gone. Stage 6 on 5 January saw 88 trams withdrawn from New Cross depot and 21 from Norwood. Routes 48, 52, 54, 74, 78 and all night 5 were replaced by bus routes 48, 149, 69, 179, 178 and all night 285. The West End terminus of Victoria saw trams no more. Vauxhall Bridge Road here was so wide that the replacement buses were able to turn round in the middle of the road.

A new garage, Rye Lane, in Peckham, opened with tram replacement stage 6. Although it was not on the site of a former tram depot, a permanent way store had previously been there.

Leyland was in the news at the beginning of the year when a handful of new RTLs, in red livery, was sent to the Country Area; they quickly came back to

the Central Area. Other RTLs went to Hendon, home of the prewar STDs which had worked the 13 ever since their introduction in 1937. These were still in good condition and took up work at Enfield, displacing Gs, a class which was disappearing rapidly.

The Green Line fleet was seeing its biggest transformation since the late 1930s. Production of the RF was proceeding apace and many of the prewar coaches which were being displaced — 10T10s, Qs and TFs — were demoted to bus work, sometimes in the Central Area, although only the Ts were repainted red. These in turn replaced older Ts and LT

single-deckers, although some of the latter survived into 1953. As well as wartime Guys being taken out of service, the two other classes of double-decker introduced during the war, the Bristols and the Daimlers, were also being withdrawn. A few were broken up but the great majority found homes elsewhere and often served their new owners longer than they had LT, either with their original bodies, or with new ones.

It was a curious thing that some undertakings managed to make these much maligned and allegedly ramshackle bodies last as long as the most cared for

Above left:
No 1849 of the last Q1 series of London trolleybuses heads for Twickenham. *Author's collection*

Left:
A District Line train of R silver stock emerges from the depths at Ravenscourt Park on its way to Richmond.

Above:
Former Green Line 10T10 No 598 repainted red and working route 200 from AL (Merton) Garage. *D. A. Jones*

prewar and postwar vehicles. Burton-on-Trent Corporation, for instance, bought five ex-London Gs from the Leeds dealer, W. North in November 1953 and kept the former G351 running until January 1967, 20 years and 11 months after it had first entered service from Upton Park garage. After that it was bought for preservation by John Lines. It was seen a number of times on the HCVC London to Brighton run, and is presently living happily, the only survivor of London's wartime utilities, in running order, at Cobham Museum. Not bad for a wartime reject. Other utility buses went off to the Celtic fringe, Guys to Edinburgh, Daimlers to Belfast, where both were rebodied. Some of the Daimlers came to sad endings, destroyed in the Troubles which erupted in 1968.

Three new buses, RTs 2775/6 and RTL1307, took themselves off on an 8,000-mile goodwill tour of the USA in March, returning without one mechanical failure and to an official welcome from the Minster of Transport in August. Perhaps it was they who put the idea into the heads of American entrepreneurs to import London buses and employ them on sightseeing work, a practice which continues to this day.

The night of 5-6 April saw the last trams operating though Kingsway Subway and consequently the last North London trams. Not surprisingly there were many special runs in the final days, the very last passenger carrying service being conducted, fittingly, by E3 No 185, this class having been associated with the Subway since their building 20 years earlier. The 33 was replaced by bus route 171 and the 35 by 172. The two depots concerned suffered quite different fates, Norwood being closed, while Highgate continued to provide a home for its large trolleybus fleet; indeed, it held the largest number of all, 127.

A remarkable new garage was opened and allocated about a dozen RTLs to operate route 178 (although it would eventually house over 200 vehicles). This was Stockwell. Bus garages don't usually feature in anyone's list of great architecture but Stockwell is the exception. Designed by Adie, Button and Partners, it boasted the largest expanse of roof without intermediate support anywhere in Europe. The great, sweeping reinforced concrete arches matched the great railway stations of the 19th century, and even now, more than 40 years on, Stockwell is still a beacon for the future.

The big story of 1952 was the end of the trams. This came on 5-6 July. The final six routes were the

36, 38, 40, 44, 46 and 72, all but the 46, which terminated at Southwark Bridge, negotiating that celebrated Mecca of tram enthusiasts, the Embankment. Not many of the LCC standard E1 cars were left, most of the services which Abbey Wood and New Cross depots operated being worked by the later corporation version of the E1 and the E3s and HR2s. One E1 which would live on was No 1025. This dated back to 1908 and it had been set aside for preservation in the LT collection. A unique feature of the final conversion was the use of 50-odd elderly buses — STLs. They were joined by some 'prewar' RTs, numerous RTLs which had been used to train tram drivers to drive buses, and just 15 brand new RTs.

Saturday 5 July dawned sunny and warm and the crowds were out and about everywhere between Abbey Wood, Woolwich, Eltham, Charlton, Greenwich and central London, not forgetting the Elephant and Castle. A delightful film, *No Trams to the Elephant* was in the process of recording the London tram and those who regularly rode it. There were many specials that day, the last ordinary service car being E3 No 1951 due to leave Savoy Street, Embankment on route 40 at 11.38pm and arrive at New Cross at 00.29am. In the meantime LT Chairman Lord Latham, together with nine London mayors, had left Charlton works in the appropriately numbered E3 No 1952 to greet No 1951 at New Cross depot. Not surprisingly the vast crowds threw these schedules to the winds, and in fact one more car, E3 No 187 from Eltham, was the very last London tram. Later all those cars still in New Cross depot left for the final, short journey to Penhall tramatorium, the motors finally falling silent around 03.00.

The crowds who attended were in a festive mood and while there was a nostalgic regret that something familiar had gone — Paul Jennings wrote a particularly elegant farewell in the *Observer* — most looked forward to a new era of reduced traffic congestion, safer road conditions and up-to-date, rubber-tyred comfort. For a little while all this came about, but soon the congestion was back too, and then exceeded anything the trams had caused. The absence of trams lines certainly made life easier for cyclists, but other traffic conditions conspired against them: few then worried overmuch about pollution from petrol and diesel fumes, and who would have thought that in the mid-1990s there would be hundreds of double-deck buses operating in central London, older by 10 years and more, than the HR2 and the E3 cars when they were withdrawn and broken up?

An ironic coda to all this is that London's very last electric-powered road vehicles — trolleybuses which once would have been intended to replace the trams — were delivered in 1952. These were further Q1s, identical to the earlier ones, numbered 1842-1891, LYH 842-891. Allocated to Isleworth and Fulwell depots they allowed a number of the oldest standard,

Above left:
HR2 No 1896 at Victoria. *IAL*

Below left:
Former West Ham car No 337 at Beresford Square, Woolwich. *IAL*

Above:
RT3414 and RTL1275, two 1952 deliveries, alongside RT422 of 1947 at Thornton Heath. Taken nine years later, all are changed: RT422, by then the oldest bus in LT passenger service, has a later body, RT3414 has the type of body which originally graced RT422, whilst the RTL is in green livery, having just been dispatched from Hatfield.

1953

The new towns, planned to create homes out in the country for Londoners displaced by bombing and slum clearance, were growing rapidly by the mid-1950s. The vast Harold Hill estate led to a new garage being opened at North Street, Romford while many Country Area routes were being re-organised and expanded to cope with the new business. In those days few of the houses were built with garages, storing up complications for the future when cars would line both sides of the not-very-wide residential roads, impeding the progress of buses.

Delivery of new RFs to the Central Area was completed in 1953 and large numbers then went to the Country Area. Virtually all prewar single-deckers were eliminated, including the veteran LT six-wheelers, the last of which were withdrawn from Dalston garage at the end of January 1953. They disappeared at the same time as the last 1T1s and thus no buses inherited from London General remained in service any longer. Only the 10T10s remained at the end of the year, some 30 odd at work in the Country Area and on staff duties.

A new class of single-decker entered service in 1953. This was the GS. Looking back it may seem rather extraordinary that LT had need for normal control buses as late as the mid-1950s, but 84 of these little Guy 26-seaters were thought necessary to replace the prewar C and CR classes and work the lanes and more sparsely populated regions at the outer

as well as some experimental trolleys, to be withdrawn.

On the Underground a new design of car for the Circle Line entered service. This was the R49. Most looked very like their predecessors but the 90 carriages were significantly different in that their bodies were built of aluminium alloy. This allowed a significant weight saving of over five tons for each vehicle. Built by MCCW they took up work in 1952-3. Amongst them were eight cars which looked quite different to anything previously seen and would set the pattern for the future. These were left unpainted. Remarkably no less than two tons was thus saved over a similar, painted, eight-car train, so that although the aluminium cars were more expensive to build than steel ones, they were cheaper to run.

Above:
GS42 in suitably rural surroundings at the Plough, Coldharbour in the Surrey hills. *Mark Chadwick*

Left:
STL1716 working a Coronation route tour. *Alan Cross*

limits of 55 Broadway's vast empire. The family likeness with the RF was plain enough, as was their ECW origin. Their bonnet design was based on that used on contemporary Fordson lorries, which had slightly down market connotations; if one could overlook this they were rather handsome little vehicles.

Many familiar classes were seen no more in LT by the end of the year. Apart from the Ts and LTs already mentioned, other single-deck/coach classes to disappear were the TFs, the Qs, the 9T9s, the 11T11s (thus severing the link with the old Reliance, upon whose chassis the bodies had begun their careers), the Cs and CRs. Of the double-deck fleet, the last of the austerity Gs and the Bs were withdrawn, the Ds reached near extinction and the prewar STDs were fading away rapidly, as was the short-lived SRT class.

The STL class, after the onslaught of 1950 when over half the class had disappeared, had subsequently been making something of a fight back, often replacing withdrawn austerity double-deckers. In 1952 no less than 48 had been used in the final tram replacement programme, including several of the old sit-up-and-beg variety, scarcely

Above:
TF40 now in the ownership of the London School of Economics and with its rear indicator removed at Waterloo.

Right:
C31 of Hertford (HG) garage, 28 February 1953, with some choice prewar hardware in the background, amongst which is a fabric-roofed Riley and a Morris 8. *Alan Cross*

Below:
Dunton Green garage with RTs 4525, 3496 and 3869, RF587 and 568.

newer than many of the trams and, some opined, rather less comfortable. However with the austerity classes virtually extinct and no let up in the delivery of new RTs and RTLs, 1953 saw STL numbers decline from 508 to 223. The last overhauls and repaintings of the class, into the dreary overall red, were completed in April. By the end of the year all the lowbridge varieties of STL had gone, as had the last red and white one, the livery which best suited the class. However there was one more significant chapter to be written in their history.

1953 was Coronation year and, just as with the Festival of Britain two years earlier, a fleet of STLs was got together to operate tours of the route and cope with the huge influx of visitors to the capital for the great event. 160 members of the class, of many varieties, were used on these duties.

An innovation which greatly pleased us Croydonians was the first orbital Green Line route. This was the 725. It linked the outer Thames-side Country Area towns of Gravesend and Windsor by way of Dartford, Bromley, Croydon, Kingston, and Staines. The entire journey took 3hr 22min, but no one except a rabid enthusiast patronised the complete half circle. The value of the 725 was that it provided direct links between places which had hitherto only been connected by several changes of bus or by train journeys into and out of central London. Croydon and Kingston, for example, were now only 45min apart, Croydon to Dartford was just 4min over the hour. The 725 was deservedly popular and the following year the service frequency over most of the route was increased from one coach an hour to two. It was the first Green Line route to avoid central London.

The former D119, rebodied by Harkness and operated by Belfast Corporation, seen in Donegall Square alongside a Gux BTX trolleybus, also with a Harkness body.

Below left:
STLs and Gs on the scrap line at Charlton. *IAL*

1954

1954 saw a number of lasts — and a first of great import. Most significantly it saw the delivery — although not entry — into service of the last RTs and RTLs. However, before we reach those momentous events, Merton and Sutton garages, long the homes, or so it seemed to us bus spotters, of the D class, said goodbye to their last Daimlers. The older, prewar STD class continued to operate out of Hendon garage until June, while the very much newer SRT class operated its last journeys, from Cricklewood garage, during July.

Throughout the early part of 1954 the numbers of the prewar STL class had been steadily declining until by mid-June they were operating just one Central Area route, the 101 out of Upton Park, although there were still a number spread about the Country Area. At peak times the 101 was London's most frequent route with 64 buses working through east London from Wanstead to the Thames at North Woolwich, a terminus it shared with several trolleybus routes. RTs had begun to oust the STLs in February and on 30 June they saw off the final 14. At the same time there was a slight decrease in frequency and the tram replacement 109 became London's busiest bus route.

A month later, on 1 September, the only STLs left at work in the Country Area were the 20 postwar vehicles. Thus London's standard double-decker of the immediate prewar years, a familiar sight in West End, City, suburbs and the Home Counties for 21 years, would carry passengers no more. They were not yet quite gone from the streets of London for they were still of use as trainers and as staff transport, at least for a few months longer.

Below:
Morden station forecourt with STL1813 of Sutton (A) garage, a wartime D from Merton (AL) and a postwar Park Royal-bodied D182-281 series Daimler from Sutton garage. *D. A. Jones*

Left:
The former Country Area front-entrance STL1494 was converted to a tree lopper; here it's parked on the forecourt of Thornton Heath Garage.

Below:
A pair of RTs, 2063 leading, enjoying a day out at the the seaside beside Ramsgate Harbour, and a selection of pre and postwar East Kent Leyland Tiger coaches with bodies, like RT2063, by Park Royal. *Author's collection*

Right:
Shiny new RT4763 of 1954 vintage based at Godstone garage, turns beneath the trolleybus wires at West Croydon and sets off on its long journey southwards to Sussex and the Ashdown Forest.

At the same time as the end of the prewar STL the last prewar single-decker, the 10T10, ended its passenger service in London, the final Country Area examples being withdrawn. Again it would last a little longer as staff transport. No sooner had the 10T10s gone than they were followed by the first postwar Ts, some of the 14T12s based at Norbiton. Only eight years old and far from worn out, although they looked no more modern than the prewar ex-coaches, they went because they were victims of a changing world. Car ownership was increasing, television was becoming a real factor in keeping people at home in the evenings, LT in an era of full employment was finding it increasingly difficult in recruiting and holding on to staff: all of which meant fewer buses were needed.

Another result of this decline was that many new RTs and RTLs found they were not needed and went straight into store. At this late stage the first Park Royal RTs in green livery and the first batch of Weymann-bodied RTLs appeared. The RTs had bodies which had originally been fitted to SRTs (the last of this markedly unsuccessful experiment went at the end of July) while the Weymann-bodied RTLs started at 1601 and continued to 1631 — the very last of its class. It was delivered on 10 November and like its 29 predecessors it went into store. The final RT was 4794, also with a Weymann body, which arrived a day later. However the float body, from Park Royal, did not arrive until 19 November. The highest number RT was 4825. This had a Park Royal body and it entered service from Cricklewood garage on 29 March.

Thus construction of the RT family, the most standardised example of bus production ever seen or likely to be seen in this country, was over. Its grand total, AEC and Leyland, was 6,805. Sadly, and ominously, no fewer than 144 of the newest example were not immediately needed. They were expected to be required for future growth and were hidden away, chiefly at Garston and Loughton garages, although I also came across a batch of RTLs, mounted on wooden blocks and without tyres, at Reigate.

In April LT announced that its trolleybus fleet, the largest in the world, was doomed and that replacement by diesel buses would start in four years time. The large majority of its vehicles were of prewar or early wartime origin and had outlived their motorbus contemporaries. Nevertheless they seemed in perfectly sound condition and did not look dated. The main problem was that new trolleybuses were vastly more expensive than diesel buses and, environmental concerns being of much lower priority to most people than they are today, the decision was generally seen as inevitable.

The last relic from a long vanished time, an NS canteen, was withdrawn in 1954. One which survived into the 1950s was 2295 which sat beside Chelsham garage. I knew it well but somehow took it for granted. Looking back it seems extraordinary that I should have done so, for the contrast between it and the shiny green RTs which had just been delivered was as great as that between, say, the first underfloor-engined coaches and canvas-roofed charabancs.

In the mid-1950s no great fuss was made of old buses as they disappeared and complete classes could vanish without ceremony, witness the end of the celebrated STLs and the 10T10s, but there was no shortage of publicity for *the* event of 1954. This was the appearance at the Commercial Motor Show of the

first Routemaster. Hundreds of RMs are still with us, millions of words have been written about this celebrated vehicle, and it has exceeded both the length of service and the fame of the RT, so there is no need for a description of it here. But it's worth commenting that the RM was rather less favourably received than its predecessor, that many modifications were made before it entered production and that while it contained a number of advanced features, it was also in some respects old-fashioned in 1954, and even more so when it did finally enter production.

1955

1955 was a gloomy year for LT. Passenger numbers were declining and cuts in double and single-deck motorbus and trolleybus routes were made in February. The summer programme in the Central Area brought about more cuts at the beginning of May, and although there was still plenty of extra recreational business on Sundays, this also was substantially down on the previous year. Less than a month later more reductions meant that overall scheduled Central Area bus and trolley services were down 5.25 per cent on those of six months earlier.

A number of strikes resulted, the men worried that their earnings, and even possibly their livelihoods, were under threat; at this stage they didn't last long but they were a warning of what was to come.

Inevitably these cuts meant many buses were withdrawn, permanently, from service. A number of the older trolleybuses, the experimental ones and all the surviving non-standard postwar double-decker motorbuses — G436, the all-Leyland PD1 STDs and the 18STL20s — had gone by the beginning of the summer. Not only this but the 'prewar' RTs now

began to be taken out of service. For some time it had been the practice to place a number of them in the training fleet halfway through their overhaul cycle; now many more were to serve permanently in this capacity, often for a number of years. Some were sold to other operators, while RT59 became the very first of its class to be scrapped. The very last to operate in the Central Area, appropriately from Chelverton Road, Putney, came off the road on 25 May. However seven of the class rather unexpectedly reappeared in the Country Area. A bridge at Broxbourne on the 327 route was unable to bear the weight of the postwar RT — up to then the postwar STLs had worked over it — so a batch of 2RTs, each one 15cwt lighter than its postwar brethren, was repainted green and sent to Hertford garage.

The postwar STLs and STDs not surprisingly soon found buyers and all worked for their new owners for many years. The demotion of the 2RTs to the training fleet meant that they could replace the fleet's mainstay — prewar STLs, which could now be disposed of. Most garages usually had at least one, sometimes more, STLs on its books and I used to cycle around the local ones in the evenings or at weekends ferreting them out. Most were roof number box types with DGX or DLU registrations, although there were a number of slightly earlier CXXs as well as the occasional sit-up-and-beg veteran. June saw the last of them withdrawn.

I had not expected to see a 10T10 again but one April evening I was greatly surprised when T631 went bustling up Purley Way with a load of homeward-bound LTE employees on its way from Chiswick Works to Reigate. By this time I had acquired an unreliable BSA Bantam and a couple of weeks later I managed to pursue it as far as Reigate where I was able to photograph T613 and a brother

parked outside the garage. Very soon both these and all other remaining 10T10s had gone.

So heavy were the three lots of service cuts in 1955 that, following on the withdrawal of the 'prewar' 2RTs, the very first postwar ones went. The ones chosen were the least standard, the Cravens. Fifty were delicensed on 1 June, although a number reappeared briefly during the two-week rail strike which began over the Whitsun Bank Holiday weekend. I had been staying in the Isle of Wight and had to make my way home by service bus from Portsmouth. Southdown PD2s got me as far as Horsham but the traffic jams were monumental. I just managed to catch the last 414, a standard green RT from Dorking garage. This was going no further than its home but a red RT on the 93 got me to Morden where another on the 118 took me as far as Mitcham Common, leaving me to walk the last three miles. Country Area service cuts were less severe than in the Central Area and 13 of the stored RTs, delivered in 1954, were put into service.

One other new bus appeared in 1955. This was the second Routemaster, RM2. Similar in appearance to RM1, it had a redesigned and rather clumsy looking front end, and the same inadequate route indicators as originally fitted to RM1. It appeared in March, and spent the rest of the year undergoing a variety of tests.

Aldenham works, originally intended to deal with Tube trains, began to operate its celebrated flow-line overhaul system, taking over work on RT-type chassis and bodies from Chiswick during 1955.

New Addington, known locally as Little Siberia, was a huge council estate on the windy slopes of the North Downs south of Croydon. It was begun just before World War 2 but was greatly expanded afterwards. One of the chief complaints of the local

inhabitants — chief of all was that they didn't want to be there — was that public transport out of the place was expensive and slow. In an effort to alleviate the latter condition, though it could do nothing about the former, LT introduced its first express bus service in August. A proportion of the 130 service was given new white on blue route blinds and boards indicating the various stopping places within the estate, whence it ran non-stop to East Croydon station. Later in 1955 Croydon also saw the introduction of the first Country Area express service when certain peak hour services on the 403 between West Croydon and Chelsham were so designated.

Above left:
The 2RTs finished passenger service in the Central Area in 1955. Some spent all their lives at Putney (AF) garage and here two in all-red livery work the special service from Southfields station to the Wimbledon tennis championships. *Alan Cross*

Left:
Former Green Line T613 and 631 used as staff transports at Reigate garage, May 1955.

Above right:
RT492, newly fitted with a non-roof-box body, at Addiscombe, September 1955.

Right:
RT3142 ready to work a 403 express service, alongside RT2504 at Chelsham garage.

1956

Probably the most interesting event of 1956 was the entry into passenger service of RM1. It was sent to Cricklewood garage in January and began work on route 2 on 8 February. The most noticeable visual difference was that it now had a standard three-piece destination display, like the RTs, except the number was on the left, rather than the right of the via display — in other words identical to STLs of the 1933-7 period. Roof number boxes were gone for good.

RM1 worked until August, the reactions of both passengers and crews being carefully noted. The seats were not as comfortable as the RT pattern: personally I found neither these nor the interior decor as pleasing as the RT design, while drivers and engineers realised there were severe front end problems. Chiswick quickly got to work and RM1 reappeared at the Lord Mayor's Show in November with a very different, and much less attractive looking front. However behind this was a more advanced engine, power steering and a much better flow of air. The Lord Mayor's Show over, RM1 went back to Chiswick for more modifications. Those unfamiliar with the parade

which London's new Lord Mayor makes each year through the City may think of it as purely a civic occasion but it's much more than this, rather more of a carnival, even if the weather can be pretty discouraging. Among the many aspects of London life which it features, transport is often prominent. In 1950, for instance, a very authentic mock up of the then new Western Region Gas Turbine locomotive appeared and LT, naturally enough, regularly takes part — as do medical and other students who can be less than totally respectful to their elders, though possibly not their betters, on parade.

The Monocoach, an experimental AEC underfloor-engined bus with a Park Royal body, which had previously done a stint with LT, reappeared from Reigate garage. Both its appearance and its registration number, NLP 635, were reminiscent of LT practice.

One-man-operation had always been a feature of the smallest buses in the fleet — the Dennis Darts, the Cubs and the GSs — but experiments had begun with RFs in 1954 and these continued with many more Country Area vehicles being added to the original four. Musical chairs proved a popular pastime within the RF fleet in 1956 with others being converted to

Left:
The experimental AEC/Park Royal Monocoach at St Albans. *IAL*

Right:
RT149 on learner duty in Piccadilly with an RT opposite and an RTW coming up behind the Morris Oxford taxi.

Below:
RM1 speeds across Waterloo Bridge whilst working from Cricklewood garage (W) on the 260.

Green Line coaches. These included the final 10 private-hire RFs, 16-25, now in a very sombre livery of green all over, six red ones and four Country Area green ones.

Very few new buses arrived, just a handful of green RTs from store; rather more disappeared. The last of the Craven RTs went in October, all but one of them quickly finding new owners; two of the first batch of TDs were sold and 41 trolleybuses went, five travelling to the other side of the world to take up work in Penang in Malaya. A seemingly insignificant event in the service fleet which decades later would have great significance for the preservation movement was the transfer of the body of RT1 to the chassis of the one Craven not to be sold, RT1420. The body had

been written off after it had been badly damaged in trying to pass under a low bridge at Norbiton. As mobile training unit 1037J and running on trade plates it remained with LT until 1978.

Two other events of great import concerned with preservation — a topic we have barely touched upon until now because, apart from the admirable LT collection, the concept barely existed — took place in 1956. The first was the celebration of the centenary of the LGOC. Nowadays we seem able to find a virtually limitless supply of anniversaries to celebrate but then such jollifications were most unusual. LT cranked up some horse-buses, some motor ones including B43, K424, NS1995 and STL445, and some current types, and drove them around Regents

Park on 16 July; five days later it displayed them on Horse Guard's Parade. In October one of the earliest of the T class, No 31, which had entered service with the LGOC early in 1930, was sold into private preservation, the very first time this had happened to a London bus.

On the Underground plans were being laid for developments on both the tube and the surface lines. On the former, design work was beginning on new rolling stock while on the latter the decision was made to institute new works and extend the electrification of the Metropolitan Line to Amersham and Chesham.

In December the Suez Crisis, brought about by the Egyptians deciding to nationalise the canal which ran through their country, and the UK and France deciding to send forces to prevent this, erupted and brought about petrol rationing. I was very aware of this for I was serving Her Majesty at the time, or rather the Adjutant of RAF Abingdon, as his typist. We, he and I that is, with the help of a few others, trained the Parachute Regiment how to fall out of aeroplanes without hurting themselves. It looked like a good many of them might be falling on top of the Egyptians and some of us clerks might have to follow in order to record the number of fezs damaged in the process, etc. However it all ground to a halt after a few days, but the petrol rationing continued and London's buses suddenly found they could get around a great deal quicker with far fewer private cars cluttering up the streets.

Above:
Former GWR '57xx' class pannier tank at Neasden depot.

1957

The dearth of new deliveries — after the extraordinary period from 1947 to 1954 when the vast RT family had been in production — continued through 1957. Just two new buses arrived, the third and fourth Routemaster prototypes. RML3 had Leyland mechanical units, hence the 'L', and a body built by Weymann at Addlestone. It was the closest yet to what the production buses would look like, although the front end was not yet finalised. RML3 arrived in July but spent the rest of the year undergoing various tests at the Leyland works and at Chiswick. For this reason it attracted little publicity.

Quite different was the reception given Routemaster No 4. This was the most distinctive of all the prototypes, being a double-deck coach. One might have thought that given the lack of success of their previous attempts at this concept — the much heralded RTC1 after its brief days of glory had ended its London career and had been sold — LT would have ceased heading up this particular avenue. However Green Line travel was increasing and they

Above:
'Prewar' RT65 on learner duties approaching Holborn.

Above:
A picture of the forecourt of Victoria station which typifies the brief period when the RT-class reigned supreme before withdrawal of standard vehicles began early in 1958.

Left:
The unique interior of a BEA RF, showing many standard LT features.

obviously thought third time lucky; up to a point, they were right.

CRL4 had, like RML3, Leyland mechanical units, but what attracted all the publicity was its handsome 55-seat body. While it followed basic Routemaster proportions and general design, it was rather more refined with nicely padded seats (although, like all Green Line ones they were still basically glorified bus ones with low backs rather than proper coach seats), luggage racks, pale green window surrounds, platform doors, polished lamp surrounds and front wheel trims, and full independent front suspension. The steering was not, however, power-assisted. The builders of the body were ECW, the nationalised Lowestoft firm which had built the GSs and the distinctive RFWs, but were otherwise chiefly associated with putting bodies on top of Bristol chassis.

Unlike the other prototypes, CRL4 went into passenger service relatively soon upon delivery. It arrived from Suffolk on 14 June and took up work from Romford garage on route 721 on 9 October. Here it ran alongside the RTs which were normally used and continued to the end of 1957. We will pick up CRL4's career subsequently; suffice to say at this stage that it saw vastly more passenger service than all the other three prototype RMs put together. Meanwhile RM2 had been repainted green and at long last went into service. It was sent in May to Reigate to work the 406; but not for long. By August it was back in red livery, despite which it was sent to Turnham Green (turn 'em green, get it?) and the following month started working the 91. RM1 began work from Cricklewood garage on the 260 on 1 March.

The petrol rationing brought about by the Suez

Crisis ended and LT produced figures showing how much faster its buses had travelled, carrying more passengers, while the roads were uncongested. The arguments about restricting the private car and its selfish use of valuable road space were hotting up.

The famous Red Rover ticket made its appearance on 12 October 1957. It cost 5s (25p) and was available on Saturdays and Sundays.

The same month the Cromwell Road air terminal opened. It was built over the District Line tracks and was a replacement for the vastly more convenient one at Waterloo which had to close because its lease ran out. LT's particular interest was that it provided the 65 coaches which linked the terminal with Heathrow airport. Although they didn't actually own them, these Park Royal-bodied 1½-deck coaches were classified 4RF4 and lived at Shepherd's Bush garage, having been transferred from the basement of Victoria. Initially each service was supposed to run in connection with a particular flight and thus all sorts of exotic destinations featured, Bulawayo or Reykjavik for example, providing an interesting contrast to Camden Town and Putney Heath, which was where the 74s, the only LT route to pass the Cromwell Road terminal, were bound. Before long, with the increase in both the size of airliners and the frequency of their departures, these destinations became meaningless and the only time I can remember travelling on this service I was assured I would not be forced to travel to Singapore, which was where the RF claimed it was headed, rather than exotic Manchester, my destination; phew, what a relief!

The 17 years of the 'prewar' RTs' passenger service came to an end in August when route 327 was diverted away from the weak bridge which

Above:
RML3 at the Bank.

Below:
Clapham Common station on the Northern Line. Although this picture was taken decades after 1957 nothing much has changed since then, when it was already something of a period piece.

necessitated their use and the final seven 2RTs entered the training fleet.

One of the worst rail accidents ever, at Lewisham on 5 December, resulted in substitute bus services for six days. The accident occured in thick fog, a phenomenon still common in London then. I was hitch-hiking home from RAF West Malling in a lorry that evening and about the same time, not far away at Sidcup, I had to get out and walk ahead of the lorry at a roundabout until I could find the turn we needed. Such conditions made it almost impossible to run public transport services. Whatever present day pollution hazards we may face, that is one which thankfully has been banished.

The first of the three experimental tube trains known as the 1956 stock, appeared in 1957 (LT always gave the number of the year when they had thought up the idea of a new train rather than when it appeared). One seven-car train was built by Metro-Cammell, one by the BRCW and one by the Gloucester RCW Co. Fluorescent lighting was standard, the car bogies had rubber suspension and livery was the now standard unpainted aluminium. Visually they were not very different, inside and out, to the 1938 stock, although the front end, which incorporated a roller destination blind, was less well proportioned. They were put to work on the Piccadilly Line and, proving successful, led to production orders for sufficient units to replace the pre-1938 stock in use on that line.

Above:
RT2119 of Reigate garage passing South Croydon. This was one of a number of not quite standard RTs, the chassis having been delivered at the beginning of 1950, whilst the body was some two years older. It was the first RT body to be repainted from red to green. RTs 2116–21 were the only ones in the 2000 series to enter service new with roof-box bodies.

1958

1958 was a very unhappy year for LT (it was all right for me, I got demobbed on 16 January). By the end of the first quarter, passenger journeys throughout the system were down by 7 per cent. Much worse was to follow. On Sunday 4 May the Transport and General Worker's Union (TGWU) called out its members and for seven weeks, until 21 June, Londoners had to make do without motorbuses, trolleybuses and Green Line coaches, the only exceptions being a motley collection of vehicles operated by an extreme political set-up calling itself the 'People's League for the Defence of Freedom'.

The industrial dispute had been rumbling on for months. After going to arbitration in February an award was proposed only to drivers and conductors in the Central Services Department, and although LT said it would consider the position of the Green Line staff this left plenty of men and women with nothing.

Above:
A former Lytham St Anne's Leyland Cheetah operated by the People's League for Freedom during the bus strike.

Right:
Stockwell's RTL1610, newly into service after four years in store is most unusually devoid of adverts and has shiny wheel discs; seen here motoring majestically over Lambeth Bridge.

At the beginning of April the TGWU gave a month's strike notice and although there were further talks the two sides could not agree and the strike began. Although there were calls by some railmen to join in, the Underground was not affected, except that demand upon its services was so great that at times it could barely cope. Most road passengers made use of British Rail trains, others came in by hired coaches and, inevitably, private car use increased dramatically.

Eventually concessions were made to the staff who had not been included in the earlier proposed deals and the strike ended on 21 June.

The aftermath of the strike was almost as dramatic as the dispute itself, if not in every respect immediately so. Many staff had left, either because they couldn't exist on strike pay or because they saw no future with a contracting LT — and remember this was the days of full employment so switching jobs was easy enough. My fellow students and I never had problems in the late 1950s and early 1960s finding vacation work, often in the transport industry. I worked at King's Cross, Victoria, Gatwick Airport and Haywards Heath stations. A friend got a job as a conductor on route 93. One morning some joker amongst the passengers rang the bell at the bottom of Wimbledon Hill while he was standing behind the bus; fortunately he was a champion miler and managed to catch it up before it reached the top of the hill!

Many passengers never returned, services were cut and fares rose. By the end of the year there were 546 fewer buses on the streets and roads of London and its suburbs. A rather extraordinary process had already started in January 1958. This was the withdrawal of the standard postwar RT. LT had simply overestimated the number of vehicles it would

Above left:
Chelsham garage with Country Area RT2256 and 2510 of 1949 and 1950 vintage respectively and RT4760 and 4741 newly into service.

Left:
RT1619 dwarfed by a Boeing Stratocruiser, Heathrow airport. *LT*

Above:
Dunton Green garage with five GSs and six RTs.

Below:
Central Area red RF335 pressed into Green Line service rounds Hyde Park Corner accompanied by a Vauxhall Wyvern of similar vintage.

need in the mid-1950s. The last built RTs and RTLs had gone straight into store, and the Craven RTs — good, modern buses with many years of service left in them — had been sold. Now it was the turn, less than four years after production of the RT ended, for it to begin the long — very long as it turned out —

process of withdrawal. The logical decision — or what seemed to be the logical decision — was taken to remove the lowest numbered RTs and RTLs. Thus RT402, and RTLs 501 and 502 had all been taken out of service before the winter was out. However, because of London's unique overhaul system, there was no guarantee that a bus which emerged from Aldenham possessed either the same chassis or body that it had gone in with. In other words it was a totally different vehicle. This sounds pretty loopy but the explanation was that LT would be losing large sums of money on the road tax with vehicles off the road for many weeks being overhauled. Thus as, say, RT624 entered the works, another RT just emerging would assume RT624's identity. Perfectly sensible, although it was something we bus spotters knew nothing about in our early days and would have been very nonplussed if we had, and it has caused all sorts of fierce arguments in the preservation era as to just which chassis, bodies and complete vehicles are still with us.

What all this meant was that selling off the nominally oldest RTs and RTLs was not as logical as it first appeared. Body changes at overhaul could

Above:
Green RT4764 of Reigate garage, RT1042 from
Leatherhead, red RT3330 from Norbiton and TD128 of
Kingston all on Kingston station forecourt.

mean that a chassis dating from 1947-8 might carry a
body dating from 1954. The HLW and HLX-
registered batches were going for overhaul at the
same time as those registered OLD and so this did
happen. Clearly it didn't make sense to sell off the
best and keep the worst and so after a time it was
decided that those buses with the oldest bodies would
go. This meant that the roof-box versions were the
first to disappear from the fleet. Ceylon purchased
vast numbers of RTs, RTLs and RTWs, but many
also stayed in Britain, a good number going to
Scotland while Bradford Corporation built up a
sizeable fleet to run alongside its trolleybuses. The
withdrawals did at last allow nearly all the stored
OLD-registered RTs and RTLs to come out of hiding
and take up work. Unlike most of their class they
entered service without adverts and so were instantly
recognisable — especially as they also retained their
polished wheel hubs and discs, features painted over
on the rest of the fleet, which made it look very
sombre. Some remained in this state for several
months, although their appearance was marred by
their paintwork — already slightly less than pristine
after four years in store — growing steadily less
bright in service. In Croydon we had such RTLs from
Chalk Farm on route 68 and green RTs from a
number of garages, notably Chelsham, Reigate and
East Grinstead.

The first batch of TDs had all gone before the
strike, while their AEC equivalents, the 14T12s,

disappeared afterwards, all having gone by the end of
November. By the end of the year the T class, dating
back to 1929, had almost vanished, just eight of the
final batch of 15T13s still being at work. Even the GS
class suffered, its operational numbers being down
from 63 to 57.

1959

The year will be remembered chiefly for the start of
the dismantling of London's trolleybus system, the
largest in the world. The trolleybus never quite caught
the imagination in the way that the tram did, perhaps
because it was never quite sure of its own identity —
it was a tram without wires, or a bus without
independent propulsion. This is not to say it didn't —
it doesn't — have its own enthusiasts and proponents.
The trolleybus can still be found abroad and is still in
production, but it can only dream of the remarkable
reversal of fortunes of the tram. Once doomed to
extinction both in England and overseas, tramways are
now fortune's favourite with a proliferation of new
systems and extensions to existing ones.

The principal *raison d'être* of the Routemaster was
to replace the trolleybus. However, although RM1
appeared in 1954, the type was still not in production
by early 1959. By this date the wisdom of such a long
period of gestation was being questioned: in a number
of respects the Routemaster seemed to be out of date,
compared, for example, with the Bristol Lodekka and
the Leyland Atlantean. The subsequent history of the
Routemaster has more than vindicated all the care put
into it; in the meantime LT had far more RTs than it
knew what to do with and so the first three trolleybus
replacement stages utilised members of the RT family.

First to go were three routes south of the river, the Bexleyheath-based 696 and 698 — isolated from the rest of the system, if only by the Woolwich Free Ferry — and Carshalton's 654. The 654 operated the oldest vehicles in the fleet, the short-wheelbase B1s, the most elderly of which dated from 1935. The changeover date was the night of 3-4 March. Many of the 23 newly overhauled RTs which were allocated to Carshalton had roof-box bodies; I never discovered if there was any particular reason for this interesting quirk.

Little over a month later, on 14-15 April, Clapton and Lea Bridge in northeast London lost their trolleybuses although most of the actual vehicles were

Above:
RT422 with a chassis dating from 1947 but a much newer body, operating in Bradford.
Author's collection

Right:
A cyclist attempts to outpace a B1 short-wheelbase trolleybus near Selhurst station.

relatively modern and lasted a little longer, migrating to other depots. Three routes, the 555, 581 and 677, were replaced by RTL-operated ones.

Stage 3, on 18-19 August, saw taken out of service London's most unusual trolleybuses, those destined for South Africa but diverted during the war to Ilford depot. Bow depot also closed, but nearly all its vehicles — mainly the N1 class dating from 1939-40 — migrated westwards to Colindale and Stonebridge. The routes which disappeared were the 661, 663, 691 and 693. RTLs and RTs were used as replacement vehicles.

The Routemaster was now at last in production. One-off RM8 had been shown at the September 1958 Commercial Motor Show. This introduced the standard front end, a most handsome design which was not only vastly better than that of the prototypes but also looked as if it might well be an AEC; this

was confirmed when the famous blue triangle reappeared later in the production run and was applied retrospectively to many earlier vehicles. The first production RMs were not used initially for trolleybus replacement but appeared mainly on central London routes and as trainers. The 8 was the very first route to receive them, from Cricklewood garage on 4 June.

They took up the work for which they had been originally designed on the night of 10-11 November when 61 went to Poplar and 16 to West Ham to replace the 567, 569 and 665 trolleybus routes. Among the trolleybus types operated by these depots was the L3. This was a chassisless design with Metro-Cammell Weymann bodies and AEC running units. Despite being 20 years old the L3s were still in fine condition and were moved several times as the system contracted, many ending up at Fulwell where they worked until the very last day of London trolleybus operation. Inevitably there were teething problems with the new RMs and many had to be taken out for short periods in order to rectify them. Nevertheless they settled down relatively quickly and rapidly became a familiar sight along the cobbled streets and amongst the cranes and lifting bridges of the London docks.

The four stages so far completed not only resulted in various replacement routes but many other motorbus routes were altered. The opportunity was taken to extend the sphere of influence formerly enjoyed by the trolleybus, essentially a suburbanite, into the heart of the West End and the City.

From time to time LT had closed garages and opened new ones: on 14 April one of the best known Country Area ones, Watford High Street, was replaced by Garston. It was possible, if eccentric, to hold a somewhat romantic image of the Country Area's vast empire and equate it with that once ruled by the Roman Empire where Croydon was the southern hub, just as Rome was the western one, and Watford in the north could be likened to Constantinople in the east. Anyone familiar with Croydon and Watford will know precisely what I mean.

One-man operation continued to spread in the Country Area, all its RFs being converted by the spring, and in the Central Area several Uxbridge and Norbiton routes went over to OMO, bringing about the withdrawal of many TDs. Some of these went abroad while I came across a number of others at Heathrow, where they carried passengers to and from the terminals to the aircraft; the first instance of an occupation which several generations of single-deckers would take up after being retired by LT. Their AEC counterpart, the 15T13, had all but disappeared, just one being scheduled for service, from Tring garage, at the end of the year.

A long way away, but of perhaps even greater significance, the last London trams were taken out of

Left:
Two roof-box RTs at West Croydon, green RT3655 of Chelsham Garage and trolleybus replacement RT1273 of Carshalton.

Below left:
RM62 in Poplar depot with L1 trolleybuses in the background. *LT*

Above:
The first electric train for Chesham seen on a crew training run at Rickmansworth on 15 August 1960; alongside is LMS Type 2MT 2-6-2T No 41284 with the Chesham shuttle composed of Ashbury stock. *IAL*

service when the Leeds system closed down on 7 November and the Felthams — sold to Leeds some nine years earlier — were withdrawn.

At the end of 1959, because of the first three trolleybus replacement stages, there were actually more RTs and RTLs scheduled for service than there had been a year earlier: 3,388 of the former against 3,266, and 1,235 of the latter against 998. The last green RTs had been taken out of store, while the RTW class was still intact.

A small, unique section of the Underground system closed in 1959 when the South Acton branch, which was worked by a single car between Acton Town and South Acton, went out of business on 2 March.

1960

1960 saw the culmination of an ambitious scheme which would extend the electrification of the Metropolitan Line beyond its Rickmansworth frontier deep into Hertfordshire and Buckinghamshire to Amersham and the Chesham branch. Beyond Rickmansworth trains to Chesham, and to Amersham and Aylesbury, had been steam-hauled, originally by the Metropolitan's own locomotives, later by LNER ones, notably the 'L1' 2-6-4Ts, and latterly by LMS 2-6-4Ts.

A few years later Poet Laureate John Betjeman made his never to be forgotten documentary *Metroland*. The door plates of Metropolitan Railway carriages were engraved with the slogan 'Live in Metroland' and the film is a wonderful evocation of a journey over the Metropolitan. It starts at the palatial refreshment rooms above Baker Street station, stops off to view 'sin and mystery' in the prototype garden suburb of St John's Wood and takes a stroll through Neasden to an excruciating ditty sung by, I think, Peter Cook, with Eric Hoskins who informs us that 92 species of birds live in the vicinity. Then it's on to the site of what was intended to be Wembley's answer to the Eiffel Tower and where many years later — yesterday afternoon to be exact — Everton beat Manchester United 1-0. After that viewers drop in on a

meeting of the finest collection of Tory ladies' hats ever seen, a snatch from the mighty Wurlitzer which once graced the Empire, Leicester Square and is now installed in the lounge of a semi-detached in Chorley Wood; then finally to the rural idyll of Quainton Road, where Metroland never quite managed to penetrate.

Until 1960 the trains operating to Rickmansworth and beyond were quite unlike any others found on the Underground system. They were a direct link with the days when the Metropolitan had ambitions to become a main line railway, linking the north of England with London, the southeast and even the Continent by way of the Channel Tunnel, for they were compartment stock, identical in layout and general appearance to those produced by the main line companies. They wore a brown livery as opposed to red or silver. The oldest dated back to Edwardian times, the most modern from the early 1930s. There were, however, some even older carriages. These were six, low-roofed vehicles, known as the Ashburys, dating from 1898-1900. They had originally been steam-hauled, had later been converted into electric multiple-units, and had then reverted to steam haulage in 1941 as push-pull units working between Chalfont, on the main line, and Chesham. The more modern, elliptical-roofed carriages either worked as multiple-units, the T stock, or were hauled by a class of Bo-Bo locomotives, dating from 1921-3.

Craven was the firm chosen to build the replacement A stock, 248 carriages being ordered in 1959, a further 216 following for the Uxbridge services. They have lasted rather longer than the Craven RTs, and are today the oldest surface stock still at work. They bore some resemblance to previous Underground cars but were of less distinctive outline, without the turned out body sides or the elaborate valences over the windows. Designed to operate as four-car units, either singly or in pairs, internally they were a compromise between traditional Underground stock which always allowed plenty of room for standing passengers, and the needs of the longer distance passenger so all the seats, bar a few tip-up ones, were higher backed than usual and arranged transversely in threes and twos.

Concurrent with the electrification extension, four-tracking was extended as far out as Watford South Junction.

The scheme was inaugurated on the night of 11-12 September, when steam working ceased on the Chesham branch and A stock also began public working to Amersham. It would be another year before steam working ceased between Rickmansworth and Aylesbury. Steam would survive for a while longer on engineering duties, the motive power being former Great Western pannier tanks, the first of which, No 7711 (L90), was transferred from British Railways in October 1956. Five of the six ancient Ashbury carriages, the oldest in ordinary regular service in the United Kingdom, went for preservation on the Bluebell Railway.

In another part of the LT empire electric power was out of favour and the removal of the trolleybus continued throughout the year. On the night of 2-3 February further inroads were made into the east London network when 34 trolleybuses were taken out of service from Walthamstow depot and no less than 80 from West Ham. The 557, 669, 685, 689 and 690

routes disappeared. Woolwich had lost its trolleybuses with the stage 1 replacement, now they were gone from the opposite bank at North Woolwich. Eleven weeks later the remaining West Ham and Walthamstow trolleys disappeared. If you wanted to sample electric traction at Stratford Broadway, once one of the busiest centres on the network, from now on you had to make do with the Central Line and the Eastern Region of British Railways, and the reminder of Tramway Avenue. Routemasters took up residence at Walthamstow and West Ham. More and more of the earlier classes of trolleybus were being wiped out, all of the Es for example. E2 No 622, had inaugurated trolleybus operation at West Ham and it performed the last journey there, almost 24 years later.

With trolleybuses gone from most of the docks area and Essex, abandonment now moved westwards. A one-off removal was that of route 611, which ran from Moorgate to the heights of Highgate Village. Special vehicles, AEC J3s with run-back brakes, were provided by Holloway depot. As with the RTs, which had replaced the similar-equipped B1s for climbing up to Crystal Palace, technology had moved on and standard motorbuses were deemed perfectly capable of dealing with the severest gradients. Route 611 had its terminus in the heart of Highgate Village, and a real village it was, and is, even if one can stand in its centre and look down the hill to the towering heights of the City offices. The replacement bus route, the 271, is today unique in that it is the only one which still repeats exactly the trolley route it took over with no diversions, extensions or reductions. What was utterly different was that it was worked in the mid-1990s by London Suburban, a later subsidiary of MTL in Merseyside, which often transferred vehicles between its London and Liverpool fleets.

The loss of route 611 made only a small dent in Holloway's allocation of 127 vehicles, more than any other London trolleybus depot. However the greatest impact of stage 7 was felt to the southwest where Hammersmith depot closed along with the three routes it operated, the 626, 628 and 630. These routes should have lasted longer but the celebrated Hammersmith Flyover, then under construction, would have necessitated quite a lot of alteration to the wiring and the trolleybus depot was also needed to house the fleet of BEA RF coaches. The 630 was my

local route and its disappearance meant no more trolleybuses in Croydon, the southernmost outpost of the network and the end of London's longest trolley ride — 77 minutes from West Croydon to 'near Willesden Junction', or 'Harlesden' as it was more prosaically known in its last days. It also meant the withdrawal of No 1721, the last prewar-designed trolleybus. This, one of the numerically small P1 class of 25 vehicles, had entered service in October 1941. That it and large numbers of the K1 and K2 classes were also now being broken up for scrap was an ominous sign of how far down the road to oblivion the London trolleybus had gone. The Routemasters which took over were provided by Shepherd's Bush garage.

The final abandonment of 1960, stage 8 in November, saw trolleybuses disappear from their westernmost terminus, Uxbridge, when the 607, worked by Hanwell depot, was replaced by the 207. Hanwell's other route, the 655, was also withdrawn. Hanwell had always been associated with the F1 class, by now the oldest vehicles in the fleet — all-Leylands delivered between March and December 1937. Route 607 had also been worked by some of the newest vehicles, the LYH-registered Q1s, which would last a little longer.

Perhaps not surprisingly the motorbus fleet experienced no great traumas during 1960, apart, of course, from the expansion of the RM class to around 500. The TD class continued to dwindle but

surprisingly there was still work for the last T. There were just three new single-deckers. They were a portent of things to come — eventually — in that they owed nothing to current LT practice being off-the-peg AEC Reliances with provincial Willowbrook bodies. They had separate entrances and exits and were bought so that this concept could be tested. Numbered RW1-3, they were the first London buses to have reversed registration numbers, 495-7 ALH. Painted in Country Area livery they entered service on route 322 from Hemel Hempstead garage in late September.

1961

1961 took the London trolleybus perilously close to extinction; although it has to be said that, small though their numbers were by December 1961, the fleet was still big by any other operator's standards. The intention had once been to keep the oldest section of the network, that operated from Fulwell and Isleworth depots, in place after all the rest had gone, because it was worked by the newest vehicles — the postwar Q1 class. However, before long it was decided to make a clean break, perhaps because they had managed to sell their postwar trolleys, and so as the new year came in the Q1 class began to be withdrawn. In batches they were sent to Poplar depot, handy for the docks, and then shipped out to Spain. One was reminded of the

Left:
Edgware's TD105.
Author's collection

Below:
Short wheelbase B2 class trolleybus
No 101 at the Hampstead Heath
terminus of route 513. *G. G. Gillham*

Right:
L3 trolleybuses Nos 1496 and 1448
peer out of Finchley depot. Lurking in
the gloom behind is an RT2 used for
driver training on conversion to
motorbuses.

last months of the trams when the most modern cars, the Felthams, were sold to Leeds, leaving older ones to take over their duties until the end came. All the Q1s, bar two, had gone by the end of the year. No 1841 donated its chassis to Imperial College Museum and its body to the scrapyard, while No 1768 joined the collection of preserved LT vehicles. K1s and K2s were drafted in to Isleworth and L3s to Fulwell; these classes were thus destined to be the last operational ones in London. Isleworth was quite a small depot with just one route to take care of, the 657, which needed 25 vehicles but Fulwell was very much bigger and a number of trolleys, other than the L3s, could be found there during 1961-2. Certainly I came across a least two L1s there which had officially been withdrawn months before.

Highgate depot, one which had always housed an unusually mixed bag of vehicles, lost most of them on 31 January-1 February when routes 513/613, 517/617, 615, 639 and 653 all disappeared, leaving just 22 vehicles to work route 627. The 653 was one of London's longest and most interesting routes, working its way northwards from Tottenham Court Road to Camden Town, then northeastwards past the Nags Head, Holloway — the busiest place in the entire network with around 4,500 trolleybus movements each weekday — and the almost as busy Manor House to Stamford Hill, where it then headed south through Clapton, Hackney and Bethnal Green to Aldgate. It was virtually the last east London route and the last to use Aldgate bus station. Two of the pleasantest parts

of London, Hampstead and Parliament Hill Fields, saw the last of the trolleybus, and two of the five routes which served the rather less sylvan North Finchley, the 517 and 617, also disappeared. The 111 Routemasters took over and a number of existing RT and RTW-operated routes were also affected, resulting in various reallocations. Individual to the last, no less than eight different classes of trolley suffered withdrawals, although not all had been allocated to Highgate.

Stage 10, on 25 March-6 April saw the last remnants of Highgate's trolleybus fleet vanish with the withdrawal of route 627. Edmonton and Wood Green also lost trolleybuses for the first time. Wood Green's route 629, which ran from Tottenham Court Road to Enfield, was replaced by the 269, operated by 39 RMs, while the Edmonton routes which were lost were the 659 and 679. Their outer terminus was Waltham Cross, the northernmost point reached by London's trolleybuses. 50 RMs from both Wood Green and Edmonton took over, although, as with practically all conversions, a number of diesel bus routes were also modified. Many K1s and K2s and the last P1s were withdrawn.

Stage 11 on 18-19 July removed the last routes from Waltham Cross, and trolleybuses disappeared from Edmonton and Stamford Hill depots with the replacement of routes 543/643, 647 and 649a. Yet more K1s and K2s and all the newer K3s were taken out of service.

Stage 12 on 7-8 November was particularly interesting for it introduced a new type of bus, one which is still almost complete and a familiar sight in central London 35 years later — an extraordinary record. This was the RML. For a long time there had been little logic in persisting with the production of a bus which was shorter than the permitted length, particularly when it was replacing vehicles of a greater capacity. So the lengthened Routemaster came into existence. An extra bay was inserted, allowing four more seats on each deck, a total of 72 in all. The windows in the new bay were shorter than those on either side, which ought to have given the RML, as it was coded (ER initially but never carried in service), a somewhat peculiar look. I can't say I ever thought it did and the RML has been around for so long now that we all take this slightly odd feature for granted. Finchley was the lucky depot (garage) to receive most of the trial batch of 24 to work route 104, which replaced the 609. The 521 (the last 500 series route), the 621 and the 641 also disappeared. The 521/621 were replaced by standard Routemaster-worked route 221 (Dinky Toys produced an RM in kit form with transfers for this route), and the 641 by the 141. Wood Green had trolleys no more but Finchley still needed nine L3s for the 645.

A second innovation at the time of stage 12 was that of lower case lettering in via blinds. A number of routes, not all ex-trolleybus ones, were so equipped and the practice gradually spread throughout the system. Although extensive tests had been carried out by LT on the legibility of upper versus lower case, the case (whoops!) for the change seems to have been more whim than practicality.

Unlike the situation 10 years earlier when the trams were on their way out, no grandiose claims were being made that the removal of trolleybuses would do wonders for traffic congestion. An ever growing problem, the introduction of one way schemes provided some relief, although it did nothing to speed up bus services, while the insistence of developers that car parks were provided underneath or alongside the tower blocks sprouting all over London simply

Below:
It had originally been intended that the RMLs would be classified as ERs but it wasn't until the 1990s that one actually appeared so styled. ER880 of London United in red and white livery with silver roof working route 9 pulls ahead of East London's RMC1456 on the 15.

Right:
The driver of Bromley's RT811 waits patiently in a traffic jam.

encouraged more and more private motorists to take up precious road space. These office blocks were to be found not only in central London, but out in the suburbs too. Croydon, for instance, became a veritable Manhattan (although it had no Woody Allen). Bus and rail services between suburbs orbitally had never been as well developed as those in and out of the City and the West End, and so more and more commuters took to their cars. This was the era of Harold Macmillan, the Swinging Sixties when we 'had never had it so good'. It was indeed a time of great optimism, tolerance and style but not one when investment in public transport was a priority, if this restricted individual freedom. Fares were increased twice and passenger numbers continued to fall.

The motorbus fleet remained, as in 1960, virtually unchanged — apart from the steady increase in the Routemaster fleet. Now over 1,000 units, it included one, RM664, turned out, like Underground and tube trains in experimental unpainted aluminium: the idea did not catch on. No more TDs disappeared and even the sole T kept working.

On 9 September passenger steam working on the Underground finished with the extension of electrification to Amersham. From then on Amersham was the terminus for LT trains, Aylesbury now being the exclusive preserve of British Railways reached from Marylebone either by way of the joint line with the Metropolitan or High Wycombe and Princes Risborough.

1962

I can scarcely recall more Arctic conditions in London than those on 2 January 1962 when I struggled through slush and snow to record the passing of four trolleybus routes operated by Finchley, Stonebridge and Colindale depots. The bulk of the snow had fallen on the previous Sunday, 31 December, and settled, but there were further flurries on Tuesday 2 January and practically every bus, Green Line and trolleybus service in and around London was affected. Paddington looked positively romantic as I watched the N1s and N2s on the 662 ease their way under the snow-clad branches of the trees surrounding the green which had served as their terminus for over 25 years. This was the last trolleybus terminus close to central London. The forecourt of Stonebridge depot, overlooked by the London Midland Region main line out of Euston, was a solid blanket of frozen snow despite the numerous trolley and motorbus services which terminated there. Stonebridge and Colindale, once the home of bespatted C class vehicles, had played host to the more modern AEC N1s and N2s, transferred from east London when their depots closed. All were withdrawn by 3 January. Along with the 662, 645, 662 and 666 all disappeared. Finchley was now an all motorbus garage; Stonebridge became one, while Colindale closed — its duties now performed by motorbuses from Edgware and Cricklewood garages. Colindale was where the trolleys met their end and so many of Stonebridge's and Finchley's vehicles made a final journey there, although others went into store for a while at Fulwell before eventually being towed to the graveyard behind Colindale depot.

Now there was just one more stage to go. The remaining routes were the 657 from Hounslow to Shepherd's Bush, worked by Isleworth depot, and six worked by Fulwell. These were the routes in Kingston area: 601 Tolworth-Twickenham, 602 The Dittons-Kingston Hill-Dittons circular, 603 Tolworth-Kingston Hill-Tolworth circular, 604 Wimbledon-Hampton Court, 605 Wimbledon-Twickenham and, finally, 667 Hampton Court-Hammersmith. Parts of the 657 and 667 covered London's first tram route

which had opened in 1901 and had been worked by electric traction longer than any other.

The evening of 8-9 May was scheduled to bring it all to an end and as the day approached more and more enthusiasts, and members of the general public, turned out to take a last ride on a London trolleybus. If many of the previous abandonments had attracted little attention, the build-up to the finale rivalled that of the trams approaching their end 10 years earlier. A nice touch saw the preserved pioneer London trolleybus, Diddler No 1, brought out some days before the end. It was posed alongside L3s and Routemasters in the forecourt of Fulwell depot, where the tram tracks, disused for the past 31 years, were still *in situ*. They became redundant when No 1 and its companions entered service.

The end was fittingly marked. No 1 did a ceremonial tour over the 657 and the 601, London's very first trolleybus route, and large crowds stood and watched all day long, the numbers increasing as night fell until the very last ceremonial runs took place. The last 657 from Isleworth was decorated with streamers, balloons and flags while, to quote the *Wimbledon Borough News*, 'London's last trolleybus was given a magnificent send off by hundreds of people. Dozens had waited for hours for the honour of a seat.' The vehicle in question was Fulwell's L3 No 1521. Although the souvenir hunters had left it less than complete, nothing irreplaceable had gone and Cohen's, who had the contract to break up it and its companions, presented it to the Historic Commercial Vehicle Club for

Right:
Green Line RMC1505 passes a Ford Prefect from the Isle of Wight on Eccleston Bridge.

preservation. It eventually found a home at Carlton
Colville, near Lowestoft, where it was restored and
can now regularly be seen at work.

In all nine London trolleybuses have survived; their
details will be found elsewhere. Of the rest the last
were rapidly broken up at Colindale, all having gone
by the end of July 1962. The final section of wiring
disappeared some two months later: the 28,000
traction poles were no longer needed, although a few
still survive today, supporting lamps or in some cases
seemingly just forgotten and left. Many of the
motorbus routes which replaced them can still be
traced, although hardly any remain unaltered and
often they have been broken into sections and are now
worked by single-deckers.

Another notable disappearance at this time was that
of the last of the Metropolitan Railway T stock trains,
the final one being taken out of service on 5 October.
Again something was left for posterity. Apart from
the five Ashbury carriages on the Bluebell Railway,
two later motor coaches were converted to double unit
sleet locomotives, while three trailer carriages, a
brake 3rd, a 3rd and a 1st moved far away to
Yorkshire where they took up work on the Keighley
and Worth Valley Railway. Two of the Bo-Bo electric
locomotives were also preserved. No 5
John Hampden is in the LT Museum at Covent
Garden while probably even better known is No 12

Sarah Siddons for she is kept in running order and
hauls specials from time to time.

Routemasters had replaced the last of the
trolleybuses but this did not bring production to an
end. By the end of the year virtually 1,300 had been
built, but new deliveries were all being stored
because of union opposition to proposals to replace
10 RTs by nine RMs on individual routes. Eventually,
LT changed its plans and went for one-for-one
substitution on central London routes. An
unspectacular start was made on 5 December when
Hounslow — not a garage one nowadays associates
with a central London route — sent out six RMs on
route 73. However a week later the entire allocation
of RTLs from Mortlake and Tottenham, which also
worked the 73, gave way. Suddenly Thames-side
West London had become RM homeland for,
alongside the Fulwell former trolleybus routes and
the 73, Putney and Stockwell received them for route
37. Next Rye Lane and Hendon replaced its RT
allocation on route 13 with RMs and finally, on
Christmas Eve, Cricklewood began putting them out
on the 16. At the weekends RMs could be seen on
several other routes. By the end of 1962 the
scheduled RT fleet had dropped by 59, and the RTL,
which was to have received the brunt of the
dismissals, by 141.

Two classes, long under threat, finally disappeared
from schedule service in 1962. First Kingston,
traditional home of the single-decker then and now,
lost its last TD, and then on 9 October the final
operational vehicle, TD124, came off route 240A and
disappeared into Edgware garage. Meanwhile in the
Country Area the single allocation of a T at Crawley
ended on 13 August when T787 was delicensed. A
class which had first appeared in 1929 had finally
gone. In actual fact 13 TDs and one T were still
owned by LT at the end of 1962 but were soon sold.
The little GSs were also finding they were no longer
in such demand and with the inauguration of the
winter programme in October, RFs took over a

number of their duties in the Country Area; Chelsham garage lost its entire allocation.

One of the reasons there were RFs to spare was yet another development in the RM story. LT decided that, despite previous failures, the prototype Routemaster coach had been a success and ordered a production batch of 68, RMC1453-1520. On 29 August the first of these went into service from Hertford and Guildford garages on routes 715 and 715A. Virtually identical in appearance to CRL4 but with double headlights and the standard production RM front end, they were splendid looking vehicles and deservedly attracted much publicity.

One further variation on the RM theme must be recorded. This is RMF1254. The front-entrance double-decker was becoming the norm throughout Britain and so a front-entrance RM made its debut at the 1962 Commercial Motor Show. Containing a

high proportion of standard RM parts, it had electrically operated jack-knife doors and seated 69 passengers. After the show it took up work, not in London but, to my utter amazement, on the 27 Shiel Road circular in Liverpool. I was a student there at the time and the 27 was one of my local routes. One evening I was waiting for the usual green PD2 when round the corner appeared this gleaming red, familiar yet utterly unfamiliar apparition. It was hoped that the RM, in one form or another, would appeal to provincial operator hence RMF1254's migration to Merseyside. It returned to London before the year was out and we will pick up its subsequent career later.